Published by

ATLANTIC

PUBLISHERS & DISTRIBUTORS (P) LTD

B-2, Vishal Enclave, Opp. Rajouri Garden,
New Delhi-110027
Phones : 25413460, 25429987, 25466842

Sales Office
7/22, Ansari Road, Darya Ganj,
New Delhi-110002
Phones : 23273880, 23275880, 23280451
Fax : 91-11-23285873
web : www.atlanticbooks.com
e-mail : info@atlanticbooks.com

ISBN 81-269-0819-X

Printed in India
at Syndicate Binders, Noida-201305

Major History Plays of Shaw
A Fresh Look

Dipankar Chakrabarti

ATLANTIC
PUBLISHERS & DISTRIBUTORS (P) LTD

Dedicated to

The sweet memory of my elder brother
Asok Chakrabarti (1969-2005)
Who had been the source of my inspiration
behind the venture

Contents

Foreword

George Bernard Shaw (1856-1950) was an Irish playwright of rare talent. His iconoclastic plays established him as the leading English language playwright of his time. A propagandist par-excellence, Shaw promoted through the medium of his unconventional plays, realism in art and socialism in politics. The word 'Shavian' has been defined as 'characteristic of Bernard Shaw'.

Dipankar Chakrabarti's book *Major History Plays of Shaw: A Fresh Look* presents a close study of Shaws' select History plays, specially, the Shavian notion of historical truth. Shaw, as it appears, does not believe that History is only a store-house of past records. He views the past critically as a step towards changing the present. For Shaw, historical truth is intensely related to the growth of his mind, his firm faith in the creed of creative evolution.

Dr. Chakrabarti's book was originally conceived as Ph.D. dissertation "Select History Plays of G.B. Shaw—A Re-examination". In this revised version of his work, GBS readers will find much to engage their attention.

Pradip Kumar Dey
Professor
Department of English
The University of Burdwan
West Bengal

Preface

As acknowledged by all conscious mind, G.B. Shaw is a literary Mohican who bestrode 'modern thought like a colossus', but he was not a historian in a popular sense. Success of his historical plays shows what he could have achieved had he devoted himself to historical drama. Subsequently, Bertolt Brecht made the Shavian concept of history plays one of the most powerful conventions of modern drama. It, therefore, becomes worthwhile to discover more precisely the nature of Shaw's achievement in the discipline of historical plays. It is with this objective that the present book has been written and it is hoped that it will prove useful to both students and teachers of English Literature. The book is infact a humble attempt to provide new insights into the mind and art of the greatest British dramatist of the twentieth century who conceived a unique notion about historical truth.

I have been fortunate in receiving help and cooperation from a large number of people in accomplishing this great task. First and foremost I express my gratitude to my teacher in the University of Burdwan, Prof. P.K. Dey, H.O.D., Dept. of English, who guided me in my work. I am also grateful to Prof. S.K. Das, Prof. Mohit K. Ray, Prof. P.K. Deb, Prof. Amitava Roy, Prof. Krishna Sen, Prof. Tapan Jyoti Banerjee of West Bengal, and Prof. R.N. Roy of Nagpur for their valuable comments and suggestions for improvement of the book. I acknowledge my debt to Dr. B.P. Mukherjee, Prof. Saroj K. Chaudhuri and Dr. P.C. Dhar for their valuable guidance and cooperation.

The quotations included in the present book have been derived from Shaw's works in the Paul-Hamlyn Edition of

Bernard Shaw—Plays and Prefaces. I have acknowledged my debt to the writers I have drawn on in the references. However, I extend my sincere apologies to those writers whose works I have referred to but inadvertently missed to acknowledge them.

I am greatly indebted to my family, specially to my father Sri Nagadhar Chakrabarti, for giving me many constructive suggestions on historical questions. I am thankful to my wife Mrs. Sonali Chakrabarty and my daughter Ms. Deepanjana who knowingly or unknowingly helped me a lot in this pursuit. Last but not least, I owe my gratitude to Dr. K.R. Gupta of Atlantic Publishers & Distributors (P) Ltd., New Delhi, for publishing my book in a record time.

Dipankar Chakrabarti

Introduction

G.B. Shaw was indisputably one of the greatest literary figures of 20th century. His influence on the three generations of English thought and behaviour was tremendous. Everybody has had his say about him, but the opinions differ widely from each other. The confusion about Shaw may be traced to various causes. He is frankly beyond the depths of many; some are repelled by his unconventional ideas; some looked askance at him in envy of his versatility. He excelled in many spheres—art, literature, philosophy, history, science, criticism, etc. Shaw left one of the largest fortunes ever earned by a writer. He had been offered the Nobel Prize for Literature, refused the Order of Merit and peerage, had a dramatic festival established for his work, helped to create the British Labour Party and became a living legend. As was in life, his death also arrested the whole civilised world. In New York, people expressed their mourning by darkening the lights of Broadway. The Australian theatre loving populace stood for two minutes' silence. The Indians adjourned their cabinet. The Swiss delivered a formal note of condolence to the British ambassador. Prominent statesmen and outstanding scholars found themselves busy to try to condense what he had meant, as social revolutionary and author. Pandit Nehru, seems to have marked the occasion when he said that G.B. Shaw was not only one of the greatest figures of the age but one who influenced the thought of vast number of human beings during two generations.

Like William Shakespeare, his name was adopted to add a new adjective to the English language, 'Shavian' is defined by the *Oxford Dictionary* as 'Characteristic of Bernard Shaw'. It appears to be a unique way of looking at life and the universe, a way conceived in the mind of an obscure Irish boy, born in the middle of nineteenth century and influencing the twentieth in a substantial way and even generations after his death.

Shaw wrote many plays on historical themes. Though they form a substantial volume of his dramatic output, Shaw's vision of history has yet, perhaps, not been sufficiently investigated. So, this effort of searching out a guideline for interpreting the unique vision of history of Shaw may prove to be a rewarding experience and may pave the way for further investigation into the mind and art of the greatest British dramatist of twentieth century.

It is evident from the present study that Shavian notion of historical truth is intensely related to the growth of his mind. It is a complex study involving almost all the phases of his making a unique historian and, therefore, any simple methodology may not help us to justify the Shavian mission behind his search for a historical truth. Hence, a synthetic methodology involving textual, biographical and historical approach is profitably employed to have the desired effect. As for the documentation procedure, the guidelines of MLA Style Sheet (New York, 1996), are strictly followed.

At the time of seeing the work at a glance, it may be felt that the cohesiveness of thought is not maintained throughout, specially in Chapter–III of the study. As the select history plays are written in different phases of Shavian mental make up, the study under reference, may apparently be seen as a discussion on discrete events denying its thematic unity. As the themes of the select plays are replete with historical events, it may, sometimes, be felt essential to analyse the story lines. Again, the shape of the plays, as we all know, are finally dictated by Shaw's fancy, a discussion on the Shavian stories about them may prove to be handy in vindicating his intent behind such deviations from the recorded history, their probable causes and the impact they invest in enhancing dramatic effect.

Chapter 1 discusses the Shavian method of interpreting history alongwith a justification for selecting the 'select plays'. However, a comprehensive discussion is there on the existing concepts of history *vis-à-vis* the Shavian notion of historic truth.

In Chapter 2 efforts have been made to find out the probable causes which influenced Shaw in developing a particular vision of history. His opposition to the prevalent socio-literary trends, his experimentations with the theory of Creative Evolution, his approach to the principal societal problems like finding out a true ruler where ruler's stamp is not misutilised and equal distribution of wealth to ensure a Classless Society, etc., appear to have a solid bearing on his mind and his forming a particular vision of history. For maintaining length, lucidity and uniformity of discussion, the Chapter is primarily divided into two broad divisions, namely "The Formative Influences" and "Shavian Response to History".

To search out the Shaviana in treating historical materials, Chapter 3 is devoted to the estimation of the select history plays. It is a long chapter wherein the three select plays *The man of Destiny, Caesar and Cleopatra* and *Saint Joan* are discussed in depth.

Chapter 4 is exclusively devoted to the study of Shaws's scintillating comedy, *In Good King Charle's Golden Days.*

The concluding Chapter is a discussion on the significant findings of the research and at the same time it is an effort to pinpoint the area for further investigations. However, the study is concentrated mainly on the major history plays of Shaw.

The Bibliography, Chronology of important dates and Index included in the book will prove useful study-aids to the readers.

1 Clio and Shaw

CLIO SINCE RENAISSANCE

History, perhaps, is one of the finest creations of human mind. Naturally enough, there had never been a dearth of sincere effort to define 'history' since the inception of the term. Hundreds of historians and thinkers, till today, have come up with their own definitions for the term and a certain amount of truth can be discerned from each definition but no definition, as is apparent, is complete in itself. Despite divergence in expression, it may commonly be postulated that history is a kind of research or inquiry. Like theology or natural science, history may also be interpreted as a special form of thought; and its nature, object, method and value can be best understood and answered by a person having experience of that form of thought. The second qualification for answering these questions is that a man should not only have experience of historical thinking but should also have reflected upon that experience. History, as we may assume, describes about human actions done in past and it proceeds by the interpretation of evidence: where evidence, perhaps, is a collective name for things which singly are called documents, and a document is a thing existing here and now, of such a kind that the historian, by thinking about it, can get answer to the questions he asked about past events. History, probably, begins by asking question about things done by men at determinate times in the past whereas the writer of legends begins by knowing something and tells what he knows. In history, expansion of evidence, perhaps, designed to make man understand what man is by telling him what man has done.

It may be hypothesized that history—proper should have four essential characteristics—

(i) that it is scientific,
(ii) that it is humanistic,
(ii) that it is rational,
(iv) that it is self-revelatory.

The fact that history as a science was a Greek invention is recorded to this day by its very name. History, as we all know, is a Greek word meaning simply an investigation or inquiry. Herodotus, who uses it the title of his work, thereby makes a literary revolution. Previous writers had been logogafoi, writers—down of current stories: the historian, say How and Wells, 'sets out to find the truth' (53). It is the use of this word, and its implications, that make Herodotus the father of History. The conversion of legend—writing into the science of history, perhaps, was not native to the Greek mind, it was a fifth-century invention, and Herodotus was, probably, the man who invented it. It is, therefore, apparent that history for Herodotus is humanistic as distinct from either mythical or theocratic. He says that his purpose as a historian is to describe the deeds of men. His end, as he describes it himself, is that these deeds shall not be forgotten by posterity. Herodotus, as is clear, does not confine his attention to bare events; he considers these events in a thoroughly humanistic manner as actions of human beings who had reasons or acting as they did: and the historian is concerned with these reasons (Collingwood: 9–17).

It is difficult to tell how far we can learn the facts of history by studying the chronicles of a particular century, but one thing is certain, that we can learn much about the century by studying properly the concepts of history which determines the nature of these chronicles. History is, as is apparent, written as a continuous narrative and integrated by creative mind, which Johan Huizinga likes to describe as, 'an imposition of form upon the past' (5).

The story of development of historiography may be viewed through Renaissance and Reformation as both the movements were interested in history though for different reasons. The Renaissance left certain fundamental tenets as justifications for the writing and reading of history.

Firstly, the Renaissance men were the eager searcher for fame for themselves and their native countries, so naturally history proved to be the most reliable guide to them. Secondly, history explains the rise and fall of nations. History, therefore, become a store house of past records. It manifests the fickleness of fortune and at the same time enables men to rise above fortune and be indifferent to it. Thirdly, because the nature of man is, more or less, unchangeable and like cause produce like effect remained a valid notion. Thucydides boldly proclaimed that he toiled to give a replica of exact happening for providing a true picture and he wrote of those events which may be expected to happen, thereafter, in the order of human beings: history was, as is apparent, used for helping man prognosticate the future more accurately. He was in favour of putting into the mouths of his characters, 'the statements proper to the occasion...to give the general purport of what was actually said' (576). Aristotle and Sidney provided two plausible justifications for the distortion of historical facts by the authors. Aristotle opines that reality ought to be used as foundation stone of a drama. All realities are, usually, believable. In a historical drama, only the believable realities are to be used. If a historical situation will not seem probable to an audience, Aristotle supports to 'invent' (Lemon: 155), a situation that will seem probable, even if it is not 'literally accurate' (156). Such inventions, in Sidney's consideration, is a moral duty of the author. In his opinion, an author's prime duty is to draw an ideal world, in which the moral law determines the fates of the characters and in which each detail is calculated to improve the reader. It is quite obvious that Sidney was not arguing for a narrow literary didacticism. He was of the opinion that literature ought to reflect moral law. To be very much precised, Aristotle and Sidney both opine that historical accuracy as a literary determinant ought not to override other possible literary determinants. An author must choose between literal historical accuracy either the effectiveness of a passage or its thematic value, even at the cost of historical accuracy.

Barclay following the footsteps of Lathrop, states that history shows the laws of God and man maintained, vice and viciousmen corrected, virtue and virtuousmen rewarded and exalted. And he adds that the reading of history seems to aid in bringing men to a knowledge of and a contempt for the transitory pleasure and the misery of the uncertain life. Histories, Amiot said are the best teachers—because an 'historie is an orderly register of notable things, done, or happened in time past, to mainteyne the continuall remembrance of them, and to serve for the instruction of them to come' (Lathrop: 81–84). Supporting the Reformation theories of historiography by strengthening the providence of God overall, Blundeville told:

> 'Histories be made of deeds done by a publique weale, or agaynst a publique weale, and such deeds be eyther deeds of warre, of peace, or else of sedition and conspiracie' (B 1–2). In his view history only chronicles, the life of those individuals who can provide the examplary honesty by following virtue and aschewing vice. The approach to such biographical study it is significant to note, should in Blundeville's estimation be made with due awareness that man's fate is controlled both by outside force or destiny and by his own character.

We all know that history as a dramatic genre grew in propularity during the last half of the Sixteenth century. In time of discussing the historical plays of Shakespeare, S.T. Coleridge framed a definition to fit the genre as:

> 'In order that a drama my be properly historical, it is necessary that it should be the history of the people to whom it is addressed.... It takes, therefore, that part of real history which is least known, and infuses a principle of life and organisation into the naked facts and makes them all the framework of an animated whole' (160-161).

In his opinion, history play is a dramatic genre mainly useful for strengthening the patriotic feeling. But it was Schelling who for the first time recognised that the history play was more closely affiliated with the historical literature than with other verities of drama. The basic of his notion was also deeply rooted in the feeling of patriotism as the progenitor of the genre. He, however, recognised two groups of history plays: those centering about history and historical personage, and those dealing with legendary history, or at least involving a more or less conscious deviation from history (Schelling: 297-351). Schelling, as is apparent, could not define the history play and preferred to describe its various forms rather than to confine it in any formula. He grouped them as plays of mixed type, biographical plays, histories of tragic type, romanticised treatment of history and plays of national feeling and philosophy.

Like other literary genres the histories, also could not stand beyond criticism and personal feeling of the reputed critics. Cicero advanced the claim of history over philosophy and poetry:

> 'History vero testis temporum, lux veritatis, vita memoriae, magistra vitae, nuntia vetutatis, qua voce alia, nisi oratoris, immortali commendatur' (222).

But the summary of the book *De Orator* helps us framing a favourable outline about this dramatic genre. The postulations, from the book, may be classed as under:

1. Historian should tell the truth without partiality or malice.
2. There should be a well-knit story with diction.
3. It should chronicle only the valid events and documents, and
4. Individual actors of importance should be described in detail and in stylish language.

To establish his point, Cicero put the instances of Herodotus, Thucydides, Xenophone, Callisthenes and Timaeus—the exponents of rhetoric school of history. But according to Aristotle's *Poetics*, the distinction between historian and poet dose not rest in the one writing prose and the other verse. In his consideration if the entire work of Herodotus was written in verse it could not give us the taste of poetry, it could have remained, as it is today, a species of history, because, poetry is something more philosophical and of graver importance than history. In another context, Aristotle also explained that a drama, like epic poem, is based on the single and complete action but history deals with one period. The number of concurrent but disconnected inclusion can never be the matter of great importance. Among the other Renaissance writers (Aristotle and Cicero), Quintilian had given a straight-forward statement about historical literature. In his opinion history has a certain affinity to poetry and may be regarded as a kind of prose—poem, while it is written for the purpose of narrative, not of proof and designed from the beginning to the end not for immediate effect; but to record events for the benefit of posterity and to win glory for its author. To avoid monotony of narrative it is, however, 'occasionally permissible to borrow the graces of history to embellish our digression' (21). He was, as is apparent, in favour of declaring historical narrative as an exposition of actual fact.

History, thus, brought to the Renaissance men an awareness of the usefulness of history and provided models for historical writing. Most importantly, they influenced the concept of history as a fit form of creative writing, opposed to the idea of history as a set of records.

Francis Bacon narrated history as one of the three parts of learning along with poetry and philosophy (fol. 10^{v}). He divided history in three main streams—'Memorialls, Perfit histories and Antiquities'. Again, he subdivided the perfit history in three more groups which were meant to represent Time, Person and Action and were accordingly called Chronicle, Lives and Narration or Relations (fol. 11^{r}).

Roger Ascham, perhaps, truly saw the place of More in the history of English historical writing. After a thorough examination of all questions about history he with Sir Robert Asteley formulated a standard for the judgement of history. From his analysis, history for literary purpose may be judged as:

(i) ...to write nothing false.

(ii) to be bold to say any truth.

(iii) to marke diligently the cause, counsel, actes and issues in all great attempts.

(iv) of euery issue, to note some general lesson of wisedom and warines for lyke matters in tyme to come.

(v) [to use diligence] to keping truly the order of time.

(vi) [to describe] lively, both the site of places and the nature of persons not onely for the outward shape of the body: but also for the inward disposition of the mynde (Campbell: 31). This inward disposition of the mind, perhaps, had given history the necessary turn for its becoming a literary genre.

From Stephen Gosson's *Apologie of the School of Abuse* to Philip Sidney's *Apologie for Poetry*, we may record a tug of war for supremacy between history and poetry. Both Agrippa and Puttenham put their toils to have happy compromise. But, even through their diversified opinions one thing is, as is apparent, established and that is historical literature to be considered as a separate field of literary study. In the end, as Smith opines, Puttenham's *Poesie Historicall* could establish a 'happy union between poetry and history' (42). He, as we may say, nevertheless put any straight-jacket upon history, for he divided histories into those that are wholly true, those that are wholly false and those that contain a mixture of true and false. The best known defense of historical poetry as represented in historical plays was, perhaps, offered by Thomas Heywood, and he eventually extended history beyond domestic level.

Croiset, a historian of Greek literature, perhaps, for the first time opined that history stands for a 'literary revolution' (589). Schelling, in the subsequent time re-soilised the notion in modern European environment and tried to establish that the English Chronicle play was closer in its affiliation to the wealth of historical literature in verse and prose which was springing up about it than to other varieties of the drama. The logic, as we may understand, may not be a sufficient ground for considering history play as a separate genre from comedy and tragedy. It is, as we may assume, still a drama, but it can not be understood by studying alone its dramatic technique. Instead, it may rather be studied as a form of art which selected and used its subject-matter for the purpose universally accepted as appropriate.

CLIO TILL TODAY

With this brief account of the concepts of history till the Renaissance, we may step forward to examine the current notions of history *vis-à-vis* the Shavian method of interpreting history by the application of present day attitudes and modes of expression to medieval or ancient situations and characters. It is often said that the facts of history are always refracted through the mind of the historian, and naturally enough, personal temperament, experience, conviction and environment of the time and place are the important determinants of historical truth. Charles Wayland Lightbody contributes to the corollary by favouring the impossibility of any final value judgment of time or history and of the shifting mind of the judges (33). It is apparent that an affinity for any such formula may help generate a new history every day denying the universal acceptability of historical events. Again, we know that the facts of history may not exist in pure form but this indulgence should not be utilised to add personal impurities to the solid facts of history. E.H. Carr opines that new vistas, new angles of vision constantly appear as the 'procession'—and the historian with it—moves along. The historian is a part of history (30). The historian, as is apparent, places himself in the centre of the procession and he, as is natural, determines his angle of vision over the past. This truism is not less true when the period treated by the historian is remote from his own time (Carr: 30). Even in this guideline, there remains a probability to air individual opinion on a specific historical event denying objective outlook. Carl G. Gustovson opines that a historian can not avoid portraying history according to his personal valuation of it, and also '...if we would be understood by his contemporaries, he must clothe his thought in the distinctive mode of expression of his own age' (172). But the historian has a learned thought—not mere the likes or dislikes which, perhaps, Mr. Gustovson refers. It may safely be affirmed that all learned thoughts follow merely a straight line, so far as their credibility is concerned. But, as all historians are not alike in their bent of mind and rank, facts and aunthetic documents are to be used as solid stones basing which a historian may be allowed to knit the episodes of history. To be loyal enough to a credible range, history cannot only be an expansion of historian's imagination. The comment, 'the history we read, though based on facts, strictly speaking are not factual at all, but a series of accepted judgments' (Carr: 8), seems to be ambiguous in nature. The sets of words—'based on facts' and 'not factual at all', may create confusion. Again, judgments are, usually, accepted according to the temperament of the age. "The historians, in general, believe in the proposition—*veritas temporis filia* which means truth is the daughter of time. In other words, historians could be more objective and clear—headed if they are as far away as possible from the events they are trying to chronicle" (Ambirajan: 23).

Again, a historian may chronicle a historical event under some duress—may it be internal or external. The external factors may cover his patriotic feeling, nostalgia, fear of the authority, etc. The internal factors may cover the historian's personal feeling about an incident or for an individual. The internal factors may also be related to the way he wants to evaluate his events or persons of admiration. Even an objective historian, as we all know, has to depend on some accounts of the past to write the history of the particular period. The present historian may be objective in attitude but the documents he gathers for the purpose may be the creation of a subjective historian. As a single historian can not authentically search out all the documents of a period, there remains a probability of lack of exactitude in chronicling historical events.

In the work of Croce we, for the first time, find a complete expression of the autonomy of history. In his opinion all history is contemporary history: not in the ordinary sense of the word, where contemporary history means the history of the comparatively recent past, but in the strict sense: the consciousness of one's own activity as one actually performs it (58). History is thus the self-knowledge of the living mind. For even when the events which the historian studies are events that happened in the distant past, the conditions of their being historically known is that they should 'vibrate in the historian's mind', that is to say, that the evidence for them should be here and now before him and intelligible to him. For history, as is clear from the notion, is not contained in books or documents; it lives only, as a present interest and pursuit, in the mind of the historian when he criticises and interprets those documents, and by so doing relives for himself the state of mind into which he inquires. Philological history, in Croce's opinion, can only be considered as a special type of pseudo-history. A misconception may lead us to believe that history consists in accepting and preserving testimony, and the writing of history consists in transcribing, translating, and compiling. Such work, as it appears, is useful, but it can not be called history as there is no criticism, no interpretation, no reliving of past experience in one's own mind. It is mere learning or scholarship. But it is possible, in exaggerated reaction against the claims of learning to be regarded as identical with history, to run to the other extreme. What the mere scholar lacks is, perhaps, living experience. By itself, as it appears, this living experience is mere feeling or passion; and a one-sided insistence on feeling or passion produces a second type of pseudo-history, romantic or poetical history, whose true purpose, perhaps, is not to discover the truth about the past but to express the author's feeling towards it: patriotic history, partisan history, history inspired by liberal or humanitarian or socialistic ideals; in general, all history whose function is to express either the historian's love and admiration for his subject, or else his hatred and contempt for it: 'writing it up' or 'debunking it'. And in this context Croce points out that whenever historians indulge in conjecture or permit themselves to assert mere possibilities they are in fact giving way to the temptation of poeticising or romanticising history: they are going beyond what the evidence proves and expressing their own personal feeling by permitting themselves to believe what they would like to believe. Genuine history, as Croce affirms, has no room for the merely probable or the merely possible; all it permits the historian to assert is what the evidence before him obliges him to assert (Collingwood: 201–204).

It may be argued that narratives about history—such as those of the contemporary theorists of history namely Hayden White and others—also serve to construct or separate a past from a supposedly more enlightened present. Enlightenment history, as we all know, was characterised by a feeling that the Age of Reason was a final and liberal detachment from the error and superstitions of the past. Enlightenment thinkers saw their own post-Revolutionary present as liberation from a previous history which uniformly depicted as a series of injustices and prejudices. This specific sense of history, in many ways, appears to be a more secular phenomenon. Reason, rather than faith, became the guiding principle of human life. The order of the world was no longer seen as preordained justified by God's immutable law. An emphasis on historical change was entwined with a liberal humanism which declared the possibility of progress and rejected any present historical condition as either inevitable or insurmountable. A sense of history as meaningful was, according to Kant, part of the character of reason. History was seen by Kant and others to be inherently, rational. History proceeded as a series of breaks with a past in a movement towards emancipation and improvement.

A number of recent studies which reflect on the uses and construction of history can not but help positing the present as at least disburdened of the myth of history as some unproblematically given fact. The figure of Hegel—the philosopher who saw reason as history—operates as something like a necessary figure in most accounts of historiography. 'History prior to Hegel, White argues, saw the past as mere error, contingency and series of events' (Claire: 4-5). Only with Hegelian history does the past possess its own specific form of truth. Truth becomes dependent upon historical context, while history is not just a series of events but now forms a context, horizon or world according to which events, meaning and truth are explained. For a Marxist, following Hegel's insight of relative truth of previous historical representations, the existential theory of angst would be true in so far as it accurately represents the lived alienation of the historical moment. But it may be considered as an act of false consciousness to represent such alienation as necessary or universal. Again, the work of literature might be seen as ideological in so far as it takes a particular historical moment—post war capitalist Europe—and universalises or naturalises that form of life as a representation of an essential and invariant human condition. Such interpretation of history and historical representation as just described rely upon some ultimate historical end in order to read the deep or true historical meaning behind the ideological representations of the past. Even the non-Marxist reactions against the totalising narrative of Hegelian history, did not depart significantly from the idea of historically specific cultural consciousness. German thinker Wilhem Dilthey, in his book *Introduction to the Science of Mind*, argued that historical study required empathy on the part of the historian and, in fact, truth was historically relative; there simply was no trans-historical standard from which the historian could judge the representations of past cultures. Therefore, no ultimate truth or reality could be gained or revealed through the study of history. The historian's task would always be conditioned and delimited by his or her own historical position which would not in itself permit of ultimate explanation. History could increase understanding of one's culture by revealing its difference or specificity; but in so far as history was the final court of appeal, the first and the last word of human life, it could no longer be used to lead to some higher enlightened truth.

This radical historical relativism was, perhaps, an attempt to understand cultures on their own terms and not according to some predetermined set of values, such as Hegel's reason or Marx's theory of economic development. Historicism of this type presented a challenge, as we may say, to the interpretive enterprise. The act of encounter or empathy was seen as inherently valuable; but it was also important that the specificity of the past be retained. Because the past was different it would demand interpretation, but this *hermeneutic leap* should not be a reduction of the difference of the past. The idea that human life was nothing other than historical differentiation was seen as a way of overcoming the limits of the present. But the difference of the past was understood within a single horizon—history—while different periods were still seen as integrated wholes; the world-view was no longer a 'reflection', but it was seen as a coherent cultural totality which delimited the possibilities of experience within a culture. While there was no brute reality seen as prior to, or determinant of, this world-view, life was apprehended as an examinable cultural whole which could be interpreted, described and reawakened by historians in a subsequent culture.

While Dilthey's version of historicism may have had no direct effect on English literary studies, the practice of historicism, in contradistinction to a Marxist explanatory or demystificatory model, has usually been the only form other than Marxism undertaken by literary historical inquiry. Indebted firmly to a nineteenth century historiography of interpretation such non-Marxist studies in literary history have, as one can assume, intersected with the 'history of ideas' and have set as their goal descriptions of 'wholes' such as 'the Elizabethan world-picture', 'the eighteenth century background', 'the age of revolution' and even 'post-modernism' While not locating literature within its own autonomous historical development, in the manner of critics like Bloom and Abrams, these histories of ideas see the text as part of a culture and as expressing that culture in the way that a historical document reveals forms of life. A traditional example is the series of studies by Basil Willey, who locates literary works within a general background of ideas. But there are more recent, and influential, examples which argue that works can be understood by referring them to a set of background assumptions which characterises a historical epoch. Jurgen Habermas, for example, explains post-structuralism as development of the ideas of Nietzsche, Heidegger and Bataille. The position of writers like Derrida and Foucault, he argues can be explained by situating them within modernity. But for Habermas, this historical picture is one of the texts and ideas; the authors he locates are situated according to their philosophical and literary heritage. Historical understanding does not refer to events but to the development of thought. The approach of historicism and the history of ideas locates texts within a general horizon of understanding—a background, world-view or tradition without supposing that these texts can be explained by non-textual causes such as the economy, progress of technological change. Such approaches differ from Marxism in their refusal to posit any extra-historical rationale or cause, but they share with Marxism an emphasis on the meaning, unity and relevance of historical periods (Claire: 5–23).

Here also the terms 'life', 'culture', 'world-view', etc. are complex enough and may be subjectively analysed. Therefore, to get a complete definition for the terms, under reference, appear as difficult as to search out a solid definition for the term 'history'. It is evident from the above discussion that in time of interpreting a historical document, there rests a good chance for fact being mixed up with fiction. In our postulation, *History—proper may be defined as an authentic and acceptable assertion from discrete historical documents.* But in literature, two divergent factors—historical truth and artistic truth—are, in many cases, allowed to help the other mutually. Historians, sometimes, use poetry to rewrite history whereas the literati takes the assistance of history to create literature. But Shaw seems to be a unique phenomena. He, as is apparent, is doubly away from the Clio—once, perhaps, by the chronicler and then by his own calculation. By using historical people and facts, and in giving a view of them essentially of his own time, Shaw, appears to have, successfully made all his history plays laudable works of art.

CLIO IN SHAW

Shaw wrote many plays on historical themes: *The Man of Destiny, The Devil's Disciple, Caesar and Cleopatra, Androcles and the Lion, Saint Joan, In Good King Charles's Golden Days*, the trifle, *Great Catherine,* and *The Six of Calais* represent almost all phases of his long career and fall into the same category historical. Even *Geneva* is subtitled 'A fancied Page of History' a variant on the description applied to *Good King Charles*', 'A True History that Never Happened'. All classic drama if not performed in modern dress takes on a certain historical colouring, and Shaw, appears to have no objection to giving some of his plays the crispy taste of historical literature.

Among the historical works of Shaw, cited above, only four of his plays, namely, *The Man of Destiny, Caesar and Cleopatra, Saint Joan and In Good King Charles's Golden Days* can be grouped as representative Shavian histories. From the rest of his plays, broadly categorised as historical, we cannot frame a comprehensive notion about the components of Shavianism though there are ample occasional comments on history. From the major plays, on the otherhand, a definite guideline can be drawn to show Shavian growth of mind so far as his vision of history is concerned.

Shaw, as is apparent, is not concerned with historical perspective, with the past as distant and radically different from the present. The sense of genuine cultural remoteness affecting ways of thought in past is minimised by the dramatist. However ancient the costumes might be, the consciousness of the wearers is modern, they talk anachronistically, as with the fore-knowledge of modern issue. Shaw, as it appears, dealt with the familiar in the disguise of the unfamiliar. He seems to be confident to view the past critically as a step towards changing the present. The conflict in which a Joan is crushed has been going on since time prehistoric. Historical colouring is meaningful to Shaw not just as part of the carnival. Shaw had derived from Marx a sense of the value of history, of the coherent interpretation of the past as a political determinant, and is concerned with relation between man's views of the universe and his behaviour in the present.

Shaw's firm faith in the creed of Creative Evolution, as is apparent, brings him in sharp conflict with the scientific view of history which tends to explain changes in thought, politics and society in terms of immutable natural laws. The scientific historian, thus, subordinates the role of individual and minimises his greatness. A comment in the Preface to *Good King Charles's* represents an occasional Shavian claim that the history in his plays has a more scientific value:

> "The 'histories' of Shakespeare are chronicles dramatized; and my own chief historical plays, *Caesar and Cleopatra* and *Saint Joan*, are fully documented chronicle plays of his type. Familiarity with them would get a student safely through examination papers on their period" (887). Apart from the characteristic scornful asides on formal education, this indicates the rules of the game which Shaw, perhaps, only subconsciously recognised as necessary disciplines. In *Caesar and Cleopatra*, for example, history is the basis of the episode chosen for representation. Caesar, as Latin

> author recalling the Gallic Wars, was only too well known in the classroom and now more congenial in an actor's impersonation. The references back to the death of Pompey and forward to the assassination of the Ides of March and the story of Cleopatra and Antony are among the odds and ends of universal education that stick in most minds. The business of Cleopatra hiding in the carpet, a picturesque anecdote that Shakespeare found in Plutarch, like the miracles of Joan's identification of the Dauphin or the changing of the wind before Orleans, is typical of legendary history, an aspect of folk tradition tenaciously defiant of scientific questioning.

Shaw, probably, exploits all the devices of the former playwrights. He confesses that the stage tricks and suspenses and thrill and jests are the ones in vogue when he was a boy and when his grandfather was tired of them (752). But at the same time, Shaw seems to regard the course of history as flexible and subject to salutary modification by the well meaning human will. Unfortunately, great men are rare and intermittent is the progress of human race. Shaw's faith in the greatness of individual heroes makes him reject the deterministic approach to history which implies a process of evolution towards a predetermined goal in which a greatman plays a very limited part. Moreover, Shaw considers it important that historical figures should be made more intelligible to themselves, for by no other means can they be made intelligible to the audience. He says that Saint Joan would be unintelligible if he had not endowed his characters with enough of this consciousness to enable them to explain their attitudes to the twentieth century. The Shavian method of interpreting history may not be called improper. E.H. Carr says that the facts of history do not and can not exist in a pure form. The historian is a part of history and now-a-days we are less obsessed by the demand of accuracy and more interested in interpreting facts (30). 'A system of historical knowledge which is all embracing and final for all times, is in contradiction to the fundamental laws of dialectical thinking (Renier: 207).

Shaw's method is, thus, a Shavian interpretation of evidence. Therefore, he may not place a historical figure in the centre of historical forces. He, rather, places the historical figures in imaginary situations like the encounter between the Man of Destiny and the Strange Lady. His emphasis is on character issuing in action, no matter whether the action has a historical basis or not. Sometimes he infuses into the historical character something of himself or invests him with certain qualities he may not possess. Charles—the Second's view on education, the English race, the choice of rulers are the views of Shaw himself; Caesar's complete immunity from the passion of vengeance or the imperious call of sex are a part of Shaw's interpretation. Some historians may object, but fictional delineation of people who shaped the destiny of their generations includes many factors of which historians can not claim to be the sole judges (Roy: 9).

2 Making of a Unique Historian

A. FORMATIVE INFLUENCES

Early Family Background

G.B. Shaw was born in Dublin on July 26, 1856. His father George Carr Shaw was an easy-going good natured man but was equally incompetent both in service and business. He was classed as a teetotaller on principle and a hard drinker by instinct. The young Shaw had a belief that the true basis of human character lies in the depth of the instinct. His Douglas in *The Irrational Knot* is, thus, free to utter: 'instinct is better and truer than intellect'.

George Carr Shaw was a man of ignorance so far as the university education was concerned. Shaw has humorously admitted that he has seen his father reading anything but the newspaper. He had an acquaintance with the works of Sir Walter Scott and other popular classics and he always encouraged his son to be acquainted with the same, to frequent the National Gallery and to attend the theatre and the opera. It seems that by getting the right impulse from his father young Shaw haunted the Dublin National Gallery so often that at fifteen he was considerably acquainted with Italian and Flemish painters and was able to recognise their works at a glance. A critic of art in Shaw formed its embryo here.

George Carr Shaw had a passion for comic anti-climax which Shaw inherited and loved to include in his plays. From the lifestyle of Carr Shaw, it appears that he was not a devout Christian. Rather he was a nihilist or rather a secularist *vis-a-vis* religion. We find a taste of his mind regarding religion in his advice to his son when he told his son that the Bible was a literary and historical masterpiece and ended by adding, with an air of perfect fairness, that the worst enemy of religion could say no worse of the Bible than that 'it was the damnest parcel of lies ever written' (Adams: 14). Later Shaw also expressed his gratitude for his father by telling: 'He was papa in the fullest sense always; and the dynamic Lee got none of the affection papa inspired' (89). We may say that Shaw's father, in his own ways, made the son a teetotaller, created his interest in art and literature, and transmitted to him his gift of anti-climax.

Shaw's mother Lucinda Elizabeth, whom he described as 'a bohemian anarchist with lady like habits' (14), seems to have neglected her children, partly through inefficiency but also because she was determined that they should not be nagged and bullied as she had been as a child. Having no taste or talent for domesticity she left the household utterly neglected. On the other hand, George Carr Shaw also preferred the frequent drinking bouts more than taking care of the family. As it mostly happen in a broken family, child Shaw was starved of affection and parental care and it left a deep and dark impression on his mind. In his letter to Ellen Terry, at his forties, he summed up his childhood as: 'Oh, a devil of a childhood, Ellen, rich only in dreams, frightful and loveless in reality' (19). In a way of compensation young Shaw was often taken out of home by his nursemaid who, instead of exercising him in the parks, made him, in an unusual way, acquainted with slums in course of her visits to her friends there. This exposure to the life of the slum and privation left an impression on the young Shaw by way of instilling in his mind a life long hatred of poverty. It appears that this hatred of poverty culminated in the birth of a reformer in him who cherishes the dream that the poor should protest and get their right of economic liberty. Although he held his mother, officially, in affection and respect, he could not forget the miseries of his childhood. The denunciation of mothers in his plays was a natural reaction of a love-denied offspring. John Tanner's outburst against mothers, probably, has its origin in his private predicament.

His mother Lucinda Elizabeth sought salvation from an untenable domestic life in music. Shaw writes: 'My mother's salvation came through music' (14). George John Vandaleur

Lee, a music master in Dublin, discovered her 'mezzosoprano voice of extraordinary purity of tone' (14), and trained her. The Shaw family was then shifted to Hatch Street from Synge Street to live in with Lee. The environment and musical activities of the home influenced much in the making of Corno di Bassetto, Shaw's pen name. It is evident that Lee's influence on Shaw ran beyond the sphere of music. Lee had been an iconoclast who challenged established belief and refused to conform to conventions. It was Lee who taught Shaw that the world could be safely defied. Influence of Lee in setting the Shavian mind was so great that Shaw acknowledged his contribution by declaring that without Lee he would have remained a barbarian.

Shaw's maternal uncle, Walter John Gurly often stayed with them. He had an inexhaustible fund of obscene anecdotes and unprintable limericks. Shaw, in his boy days, was accustomed to listen to the conversations of Lee, Walter and his father, in which Christianity was often the subject of blasphemous jokes. This gave a bias to Shaw's innate tendency to challenge established social standards.

By infant baptism, Shaw was a member of the Protestant Episcopal Church of Ireland. At his father's desire he had to attend Sunday Schools regularly and to sing hymns and say prayers. At the age of ten he stopped Church going but he continued repeating the Lord's prayer every night at bed. In a summer evening while he was walking leisurely over Dalkey Hill he was pre-occupied by a doubt as to why he should pray every night when he did not have any faith in it. Thus was born a critical mind in him which stopped him saying prayer to Lord anymore. Shaw described this intellectual awakening as moral passion in *Man and Superman* and distinguished it from traditional conscience by its destructiveness. With the dawn of this moral passion, Shaw had become a reformer by temperament. As an iconoclast he began mentally to shatter creeds and demolish idols.

Shaw's formal education was also full of hazards. Besides taking lessons first from a governess and then from a clerical uncle he had to cross the doors of four successive schools at the attainment of ten. In his opinion these schools are just 'damnable boy prison' and attending them were sure a wastage of time. In his version, the teachers were indifferent to the young learners and he avoided the school tasks simply by never doing them. His principle of education was much influenced by his boyhood experiences. Even at a matured stage, Shaw could not sum up what the schools professed to teach. From his boyhood Shaw was a voracious reader so he could learn everything for which he had a natural interest. As his parents were uncoercive, Shaw's education was free from all sorts of restrictions. When the good boys were busy with their text books, Shaw could make him saturated with the works of William Shakespeare, Walter Scott, Bunyan, Shelley and Dicknes, and his literary and aesthetic taste ripened with phenomenal rapidity. This freedom, both at home and schools helped him gain a maturity more than his chronological age.

Shaw could not continue his schooling due to economic stringency and he was put to work as a 'junior clerk' (Shaw: 30), in a respectable Irish firm. Although his 'heart was not in the business' (*Ibid*: 30), he had to continue working there as Lee's contribution for the family was stopped. His mother could solve the problem by migrating to England with her two daughters. The superiority of women over men in. Shaw's work sprang, according to MacNulty (1), from the spectacle of his father's inefficiency in everything he did and his mother's contempt for her husband.

The young unwilling Shaw continued working in the firm and he enjoyed a step up in service from junior clerk to head cashier. His meticulous care for the firm-affair and his efficiency made him fit for the new post: 'I found no difficulty in doing the work' (Shaw: 31). His satisfied employer increased his initial salary of eighteen shilling a month to eighty shilling a month within four years of his service. But Shaw was not happy with the mode of service. He had to collect the rents from a dozen of slum houses in Dodd's Row. This was an experience which provided him with the necessary knowledge for writing his plays like, *Widower's House*. Probably, the only satisfaction he had was, that he could mix and freely argue with young men fresh from Trinity College. So naturally, he got the fair chance of sharpening his wit against theirs and to learn the proper way of holding an intellectual discourse. In art, literature and music, he had an upper hand on his University-educated friends. Proving all efforts of Mr. Townshend, from the firm's side futile, he resigned the job in March 1876, at the age of twenty and sailed for London to join his mother and sisters there.

Irish Background

G.B. Shaw was born with gifts that made him a great dramatist but his development was impeded and his idiosyncrasy is the consequence of nature as well as nurture. The turmoil of his private life shaped and haunted his artistic development. Heredity and environment worked together to produce a genius in Shaw. His father, as portrayed by Shaw, was an educated Irish Protestant gentleman having no inheritance whatsoever. It took time for Shaw to come out of the Irish traits which coloured his vision in the early part of his life. On looking out he found that two of his predecessors W.B. Yeats and James Joyce were more European than Irish in their temperament and vision. Looking in the depth of his Irish soul Shaw discovered what constitutes Irishness, Irishman's inbuilt opposition to tyranny, indomitable passion for liberty and democracy. Naturally, Shaw formed a desire to champion these Irish qualities in his work. This resulted in his becoming a propagandist who is out to propagate his own views in his inimitable style. On closer scrutiny he found that his Irish contemporaries in Dublin were a confused lot of writers devoid of a sure footing or a base. They were not sure of their artistic mission or goal. In Shaw's time the works of common-run Irish writers were marked with certain flippant futile derision and belittlement that confuses the noble and serious with the base and ludicrous (Stewart: 122). Shaw left his birthplace at an earlier age than Joyce and before he could feel throbbing of an emotional attachment in the depth of his soul. Probably, for this reason his works retain the existing social norms of Ireland along with the nobler Irish virtues.

In *Sixteen Self Sketches*, Shaw has left an impression of his exclusively clannish mind which is perceptible in the Shaw lineage. Irishmen are particularly clannish. To them family is the microcosm which blots the universe. Pride in his family lineage was so uppermost in the mind of Shaw's father George Carr Shaw who had no inheritance whatsoever but who nevertheless developed a confidence that there was an inborn virtue of gentility in all Shaw's as 'partisans of William the Conqueror'. In those days, the potent Irish families had a keen interest to have landed estates of their own or of their relatives in Ireland. It is also acknowledged that one of the members of Shaw's family had founded the Royal Bank and he had also been declared a baronet. Being the second cousin of the baronet, George Carr Shaw was privileged to hire a carriage and attend 'the Bushy Park funerals' along with some important family parties. All Shaws were essentially Protestants and snobs. This peculiar clannish heritage explains to a considerable degree the Shavian sense of snobbishness.

It appears that Shaw's religious thought was shaped by his acute Irish sensibility. In his childhood Shaw was christened by his uncle as his godfather was heavily intoxicated. This is one such incident which prompted young Shaw to nurse, though temporarily, a doubt that the Protestant gentry of Ireland was most irreligious. It dawned upon his impressionable mind that Irish Protestantism was more a political formulation than a religion-proper—'a class prejudice, a conviction that as a person the Roman Catholics are socially inferior' (Shaw: 47). The Irish Episcopal Protestants believed that the Catholics can at best go to hell after their death as the heaven is in the possession of Protestant gentry. Shaw proved himself to be a Protestant, in true sense of the term, by invoking a God of reason. He could rediscover a religious Ireland in his particular vision. Shaw dreamt that the Irishman's God does not rest in any orthodox division of the faith rather in the inherent artistic capability of the race. To propagate this vision of religion became Shaw's mission. His mother had a considerable musical talent and hence the Shaws were able to enjoy the fruitful association of other performing artists of contemporary England. His first problem as to whether God can become a good Protestant was solved. He, probably, believed that true religion is that which binds men to one another and irreligion is that which sunders.

According to the best of his belief, the essence of true religion amongst the Irish people lies in its 'musical genius and irreligion in its Churches and drawing rooms' (Shaw: 47).

Conventionally, the clannish Irish people are religious and Shaw was not an exception to that. But the only particularity about the Shavian variety of the word religion is that his was the religion neither purely Protestant nor properly Catholic but humanistic. The root of his religion was humanity. Ground was prepared by his predecessor W.B. Yeats who took to the preaching of Celtic mythology through the medium of poetry and drama. Also with the French artists drama became a religious exercise. While the French artists preferred Pagan rites and Christian liturgy for the sacrificial basis of art, Shaw chose his own goal. He was very willing to give a religious tone to his plays, but he had no idea of aping ancient ceremonials in the modern theatre. Since the theatre was a temple he enshrined the Life Force in it, but he did not insist on rites of worship (Valency: 409). It appears, the Shavian theory of Life Force did emerge from the influence of his Irish intellectual background among other influences.

The Irish have all along excelled as actors. In England, dramatists of Irish origin like Shaw and Galsworthy excelled in the writing of good and realistic plays. The psychological effects of his theatrical heritage went a long way in building up. Shaw's dramatic craftsmanship. It appears that he was born to the peculiar traits of character which an Irishman inherits by birth.

Shaw expressed his gratitude to the National Gallery of Ireland for providing a cherished asylum. It could effectively minimise the tensions of the young Shaw. He was probably the only Irishman who had ever been in it, except the Irish officials. In the making of Shavian mind the Gallery had a better influence than the 'two confiscated medieval Cathedrals so magnificently 'restored' out of the profits of the drink trade' (Shaw: 47).

The atmosphere of Ireland is congenial enough to nourish an artistic mind. From Nature, also, one can learn everything. The scenery of 'days that are over' can easily make an Irishman melancholic. Shaw held the cudgel in his own hand to uplift his down-trodden countrymen, not by joining issue with the fellow Irishmen who were bred in romance but by invoking a serious purpose and patriotism.

When the young Shaw reached London crossing the Irish channel he, seems to have, no resolution. He left Ireland, probably, because Dublin could not make him a dreamer about a bright future there. Shaw did not believe in Mac Manus's assertion that the youth must be conscious about their own talents. The Shavian effort of becoming an opera singer or a painter had been thwarted. But he did not stop his effort of writing though, he was not conscious about it. 'As to conquering London I no more dreamt of such a possibility than the poorest Irish peasant emigrant dreamt of conquering the United States' (Roy: 9). With such a bent of mind, the young Dubliner came to London to conquer the world of literature.

Intellectual Background

Shaw, after realising that there was no prospect for him in Ireland, found himself turning to his mother and joined her family in England. Though Irish men are primarily committed to their family, Shaw remembered her mother who was away in England in times of his utter desperation and need. In time of Shaw's joining his mother's family in England, the family already was crawling through a rough passage—her elder daughter has recently passed away and their pecuniary condition was equally alarming. The surviving daughter and the unfortunate mother were eking out a living with much difficulty. Shaw's arrival in this trouble-trodden family was equally embarrassing to both the parties. In London, Shaw lived with his mother and sister in a semi-detached house off the Brompton Road. The family was dependent on his mother's meager earning by teaching music and his sister's singing as a professional. Besides these, they had a small inheritance on which they could draw. An unwanted increase in family membership, without income, made the mother nurse an indifferent attitude for her son and antagonism on the part of the sister. Their attitude turned the new-comer, who sought consolation and succour, mortally shy and diffident.

Shaw's assimilation to the London society was not smooth. From his childhood Shaw had suffered a sense of social isolation in Dublin which, almost, had given birth to an inferiority complex in him; grown mainly, out of his father's habitual recourse to drinking. This was partially compensated with the arrival of Lee in their house and through music he enjoyed a tolerably good social life. The departure of Lee from the house and his mother's migration to London left young Shaw desolate and miserable. In London, he was utterly ignorant of English norms and social routine. His obsessive shyness and a sense of inferiority, acted as a hindrance so far as his assimilation to the society was concerned. But his many sided intellectualism, artistic aptitudes and burning moral passion helped him to precipitate this problem. He could overcome his shyness by assuming an outrageous air of authority in conversation by aping a boldness though he shivered in his shoes. He thus created an artificial personality and named it G.B.S. Safe under the persona of G.B.S., an iconoclast had gone on its normal course of breaking social images, playing a game with the press and public. He was first denounced and then cheerfully forgiven as a privileged Irish lunatic.

Shaw knew his mission for certain. What he saw around him appeared to be sham and hypocrisy. The world of the middle-class was full of pretension and humbug. It needs a virulent critic who could set the record straight. He was sure that critic's art was his forte.World needed fresh, bold and creative ideas to dislodge the romantic and untrue hallucination from the mind of men. Shaw was after new ideas for providing an antithesis to the existing norms and beliefs prevalent among the people. Hence, the real Shaw went into isolation, beyond the reach of gossip and scandal, haunting the British Museum, studying economics, blue books and philosophy.

But the problem of his unemployment was not over. Lee engaged him as the music critic in an unimportant weekly paper called *The Hornet* and allowed him to take half of his remuneration. But the paper died in October, 1877, putting Shaw out of work. Shortly after that, Shaw joined the Way Leave Department of the Edison Telephone Company through the recommendation of his cousin Mrs. Cashel Hoey, who was also an author of some calibre. On 1 June, 1880, the company was merged with the Bell Telephone Company where Shaw had been reinstated but he himself managed to get out of it. In search of freedom, he left the service just after the completion of his seven and a half months. The only remunerative job he did for sometime, after that, was counting votes in a by-election in Leyton which brought him a few pounds. By then, Shaw became an able-bodied pauper and remained so until 1885 and earned plenty of money directly by his pen.

In 1879, Shaw had joined a debating society name Zetetical Society. The society offered its members complete freedom of discussion, 'political, religious and sexual' (Shaw: 56). Women took an important part in the debates. The special feature of this society was that each speaker, at the conclusion of the speech could be cross-examined. This aspect, later on, helped Shaw to culminate a ready wit with grandiloquence. All the members of the society were the devoted admirers of John Stuart Mill, Charles Darwin, Malthus, Herbert Spencer, Huxley and Ingersoll. When Shaw, for the first time, went with James Lecky to the Zetetical meeting he had never spoken in public. He knew nothing about public meeting or their order. In time of delivering his first speech in the society, he acknowledged to be possessed with *an air of impudence* along with virulent arrant cowardice, nervousness and self-consciousness to a heart breaking degree. There and then he resolved to practice public speaking at every possible opportunity. Shaw, a few months later, joined Stopford Brooke's Bedford Society, along with many other societies. At all these meetings Shaw took part in the debates. Soon his nervousness was off and he became the most spontaneous speaker in the world. His gift of the gab is perceptible in most of his works.

In 1884, Shaw went to hear Henry George speak on Land Nationalisation and the Single Tax at the Non-conformist Memorial Hall in Farringdon Street. So far Shaw had never studied social questions from economic standpoint. This lecture opened his eyes to the importance of the economic root of the society. Shaw read George's *Progress and Poverty* and went to a meeting of Hyndman's Marxist Democratic Federation where he had been contemptuously dismissed as a novice for not having even a first hand acquaintance with Karl Marx's *Das Kapital.* This was a turning-point in his life. Off he went to the British Museum to read the French version of the *Das Kapital.* It converted him to socialism, provided him with a purpose and made him a revolutionary writer. For nearly twelve years he preached the gospel of Saint Marx, three times a week, at street corners and in hall, at the dock gates and at the British Association.

Within a short span of time, Shaw could realise that Hyndman's congregation of manual-working pseudo-Marxists could only provide hindrances for the progress of his ideas and naturally, he had to find ways for his freedom. Shaw's search to join a suitable organisation for propagating his new faith was over on 5th September, 1884, after joining the Fabian Society. The Society, as he recognised, was an appropriate body for airing his vision of educated middle class intelligentsia. From the point of genesis, the Fabians were somewhat otherworldly, ethical and mystical. They ceased to believe in building up of a theoretical Socialist Society with the consideration that the purpose of reorganizing society is best served by practical socialism. From his Fabian association, Shaw gained a notion that morality is an offshoot of socio-economic conditions which coloured his socialistic imaginations. In those days, his meeting with William Archer ended in a fruitful friendship, so far as Shaw's resolution for writing drama was concerned.

In 1885, William Archer, the dramatic critic, noticed Shaw in the British Museum, absorbed in *Das Kapital,* with the score of Wagner's *Tristan and Isolde* open beside it. At that time Shaw was twenty-nine and Archer was just two months junior to him. They became friends, and Archer arranged for Shaw to work as a critic. It was also resolved that they collaborate in the writing of a drama, Archer to provide the scenario and Shaw, the dialogue. By transferring a part of his journalistic work, Archer assisted Shaw to become book reviewer to the *Pall Mall Gazette* from May, 1885 to August, 1888, and art critic to *The World* from February, 1886 to May, 1889. After nine years' penury,

Shaw found himself with an income of £117 per year. In 1888, Shaw joined the nascently founded paper *The Star* as its music critic. There he wrote articles in the pseudonym of Corno di Bassetto. In 1890, he resigned from this post and worked as musical critic to *The World* till 1894. In January, 1895, Shaw accepted the post of dramatic critic at the remuneration of £6 a week from Frank Harris, the newly appointed editor of *The Saturday Review*. Here his articles made his initials G.B.S. famous throughout the theatrical world. In May 1898, Shaw resigned from *The Saturday Review*. This year was also important in the personal life of Shaw because on 1st June, 1898, he married Miss Charlotte Frances Payne Townshend. Many of Shaw's love scenes seem to have been founded on personal experiences. The first act of *The Philanderer* is a deliberate dramatisation of one of his real life happening. Blanche Satrorius in *Widower's House* and Julia Craven in *The Philanderer* are modeled on Jenny Patterson, who developed a wild fascination for Shaw.

Archer introduced him to the works of Henric Ibsen, the revolutionary Norwegian dramatist. Perhaps, this was the second turning point in Shaw's life. Shaw developed a passion for Ibsenism and took to attacking the bardolatry. Ibsen, as Shaw conceived, wrote about the philistines living in not-so-big towns, and about the kind of problems that really wrecked their every day lives. In the Shavian view, a typical Ibsen-type household can be found everywhere and in all times.The story of a *Doll's House* or of a *Ghost* is a phenomenal episode of nineteenth century middle class family. From Ibsen, Shaw got a wisdom about the ideal theme of a problem play, stage and psychological need of the audience. Now he could draw a line between what the way of life is and what it ought to be. Shaw inherited a notion from Ibsen that a stage can be seen as an ideal place for stimulating discussion, for understanding other points of view. But Shaw, as it seems, added a quality of his own—it should be a place for 'teaching by laughter and excitement as well' (Adam: 120–123).

As it appears, Ibsen underlined his moralising by tragedy whereas Shaw used comic anti-climax as a dramatic tool for the same purpose. Shaw, by means of *The Quintessense of Ibsenism*, assimilated Ibsen, in some degree, to the Shavian sphere. Shaw believed, unlike Ibsen, that the age of reason had to go its way after the age of faith. His first plays, specifically *Windowers' House* and *Mrs Warren's Profession*, were the result of experimentation with play writing in Ibsen's manner. But Ibsen also, as Shaw conceived, could not provide a perfect and permanent model of drama before the audience. In search of perfection specially, in theme and form, so far as socialistic drama was concerned, Shaw subsequently encountered John Galsworthy.

Shaw was greatly moved by the dramatic craftsmanship of Galsworthy. *The Silver Box* appeared in 1906, showed that a new dramatist had appeared, with style and attitude of his own. His aim, probably, was to create such an illusion of actual life passing on the stage as to compel the spectator to pass through an experience of his own, to think and talk and move with the people he sees thinking and talking and moving in front of him. *The Silver Box* was in fact a play of ideas. He had a humanitarian outlook on life and he strove to the best of his ability to adopt an objective attitude. Galsworthy was not sentimental in his approach and only rarely did he rely upon pathos for the effect of his scenes. He developed an excellent sense of dramatic architecture which Shaw, seems to have, borrowed in his own way. From the thematic point of view, one can easily tell that there is not a line from Galsworthy's pen that is 'bloodless' (Huang: 10), not a line that is devoid of emotion. Shaw, on the other hand, is pre-occupied with getting at facts. The fact-facing Irishman is first, a seeker for truth whilst Galsworthy is a man of feeling. There was a poet hidden in the person of Galsworthy but Shaw, perhaps, did nothing but philosophising, banishing the poet from his mind. Galsworthy's bitter realism is scrupulously wrapped up with sweet lyricism whereas Shaw used the same bitterness without a suger-coating. To counteract this lyricism in Galsworthy's characterisation, all Shaw does is to fill his characters with what he calls the Life Force, and leave them at that. Shaw's application of the *Theory of Life Force*, may also be assumed to have a root in his opposition to Galsworthy.

Being an Irishman in head and heart, Shaw, naturally had an intense interest in the Irish Revival Movement which was, from 1904 to 1910, ably pioneered by J.M. Synge. Synge turned to the speech and imagination of Irish country people to restore vitality to English drama. In his preface to *The Playboy of the Western World,* he opined that a drama must present reality enriched with pure joy. The absence of 'pure joy' in musical comedies, according to him, was the root of its decline. Shaw had been moved by Synge's motive of providing a criticism of life through comedy. But the canvas of drama for Synge was limited. In comedy he wrote only of peasants of east or west of Ireland and tragedy he limited himself further to the depiction of the elemental passions in their barest simplicity. Shaw, on the other hand, was free to choose topics from anything related to the human race. Shaw's Irish sensibility was, as it appears, better satisfied in the success of Synge as a dramatist of his clan and his sensitive insight into human nature.

Shaw's early intellectual upbringing was bounded by the materialistic considerations of a Social Democrat of the 1880's, but Goethe was an example before him. In the second part of *Faust*, Goethe had shown the possibilities of drama conceived so that the destiny of humanity could be prefigured in the fate of a single individual. Excepting the difference in magnitude there was no such hurdle to interpret the Faustian adventures as a romantic version of *The Pilgrims Progress*. Goethe's symbolism was more weighty than the sheer allegory of Bunyan. In Shaw's youth, though Goethe was very much in fashion, he revered Bunyan. More than anyone, he had inflamed the imagination of Lamartine and Hugo, and through them of a whole generation of interesting writers. It was precisely to this time that Shaw looked for a point of departure in his artistic enterprise (Valency: 406-407).

B. SHAVIAN RESPONSE TO HISTORY

Setting of Shavian mind

The nineteenth century traditional stagecraft with its elaborate spectacle, erotic intrigue and flamboyant histrionics, seems to have, had a great ordering principle in setting the

Shavian mind for trying his hand in the field of historical drama. So far as dramatic technique is concerned, Shaw could not add anything noteworthy but followed the footsteps of the former playwrights. He, as is clear, included the latest mechanical improvements for carrying on an action without impossible soliloquies and asides. His audience was trained to realise reality. They got on and off the stage without requiring four doors to a room which in real life would have only one. And as far as the story was concerned, Shaw used to prefer the traditional old ones and his characters, naturally, were the representatives from almost all the stratas of society. In the use of dramatic tools such as suspense, thrills, jest, etc., he had catholicism enough to follow the age-old conventions. His probation as a dramatic critic helped him to be acquainted with all the stage tricks prevalent in the period.

It was, probably, the bardolatry of the nineteenth century threatre which bogged down all historical plays into a stage tradition of speech in *period* English. No historical character on the Victorian stage ever talked or reasoned or acted in an every-day way, rather, they preferred to behave in a special stagey manner-one which was traditional. When the audience went to see a historical play, they did not expect to feel personally involved, or to identify themselves with the characters or their problems. They simply listened and watched but remained untouched, feeling it was more an improved history lesson than an emotional experience. But when Shaw wrote his first historical play, he broke away from the tradition and presented Napoleon as thinking and talking in the same way as the audience did. The Shavian Caesar is human enough for any man in the audience to identify with him. In *Caesar and Cleopatra,* Shaw deals with the theme of the consummation of romantic love. But as one of the three plays for Puritans, the play is supposed to be anti-erotic in nature. In course of action, Mark Antony never sets foot on the stage, he only hovers on the edges of the play. As a matter of dramatic necessity, 'the future spells the assassination of Caesar and the romance of Antony (Bentley: 78). His *Saint Joan* exploits the elaborate spectacle and the histrionics, and *In Good King Charles's Golden Days* exploits significantly the erotic aspects. Though Shaw did not entirely break away from the nineteenth century history play, he successfully 'turned for guidance to the dramatists who were his immediate predecessors and laid a heavy toll on them' (Nicoll: 197).

Shaw portrayed his historical characters on the basis of modern analogies. There is no line of demarcation between time-past and time-present. In the preface to *Saint Joan*, he flatly declares that in order to make modern audience sensible about the change in taste for methodical reasoning, mainly due to time-gap, he had to endow his medieval characters with twentieth century consciousness. All possible efforts were on to make the dramatic personae intelligible to themselves as well as to the audience. In some cases, by their speech and action, the dramatic characters had to perform dual duties, so far as the unearthing of their whole identity was concerned. To make a twentieth century audience conscious of an epoch fundamentally different from it's own, in *Saint Joan* Cauchan and Lemaiter had to make intelligible not only themselves but the Church and Inquisition. In the same way Warwick had, also, to make the feudal system intelligible, in addition to his normal action required for the progress of dramatic process. As we all understand, a real Cauchan, a Lemaiter or a Warwick could not have done this because they, in actuality, belonged to the Middle Ages and hence, naturally, unaware of the modern sophistication. But to make the characters alive, even in the twentieth century, Shaw loaded them with a modern consciousness. Shaw, claims to have, sacrificed true-to-life realism to secure sufficient veracity to justify the speech and actions of the three Shavian exponents in this drama. He collected the truths about their characters from the available documentations and his 'divine power'. He boldly declared: 'I represent these three exponents of the drama as saying are the things they actually would have said if they had known what they were really doing. And beyond this, neither drama nor history can go in my hands' (Shaw: 632). Shaw applied magic realism to interpret historical justice. It is apparent that the remote and unfamiliar world of the nineteenth century historical drama stands as a contrast to Shaw's world where contemporaneity breaks through again and again. No playwright, now-a-days, would think of trying to write a historical play in *period* English. During the last forty years, there has been a spate of naturalistic historical plays but the characters think and act and talk in twentieth century idioms (Adam: 126–128). This trend of writing pseudo-history for dramatic purpose, probably, was invented and first put into the English stage by Shaw.

But Shaw was not alone in the English theatre of the 1890's as a writer of plays who invites the society by engaging himself with controversial social and moral questions. To attack the stagnant thoughts of the period, as it appears, he had to treat his characters, even the well known historical personages, in such a way where humanistic aspiration and probability played a vital role. In 1882, William Archer, in the introduction of his *English Dramatists of Today*, had roundly condemned the shallowness and philistinism of both drama and the audience of the time. The condition, according to Archer, was like that, if a drama opened the slightest intellectual, moral or political question it is certain to fail. His allegation against the British audience is that they like to laugh always, cry sometimes, shudder now and then—but not eager to think even once. But in the 90's, a new kind of drama was developing side by side with the old. The two most prominent English dramatists of the 90's, Arthur Wing Pinero and Henry Arthur Jones, were finding audiences receptive to plays in which such subjects as the Victorian double standard in sexual morality, the plight of the fallen women, marital infidelity and female liberation were canvassed. At their best, Pinero and Jones treat such subjects with some sympathy and insight, but the plays of both the dramatists, seems to have, suffered from the same fundamental flaw,—evasiveness. However, challenging the beginning and middles of their plays may be, the end are always written with an eye to the strict boundaries of Victorian moral sympathies. Both dramatists were vulnerable to the criticism which Shaw made of Pinero in a review of *The Notorious Mrs. Ebbsmith*; that he had no idea beyond that of doing something daring and bringing down the house by running away from the consequences. The plays of Pinero and Jones thus seem to provide text-book examples of the relations which can exist between artistic form and ideological context. Whatever threat may be posed in the plays to the norms of Victorian morality, the movement of the action is invariably towards a facile and unconvincing return of the properties.

In those plays, there was as much social as dramatic criticism in Shaw's notices; for he saw in Jones's plays, which were regularly produced in the West End, the best available charms of beginning the reformation of the fashionable theatre and making it a force for cultural and social change. In the Shavian judgement, Jones was the only one of the British dramatists whose sense of the earnestness of real life has been deep enough to bring him into serious conflict with the limitation and levities of the British Theatre. In many passages in the *Saturday Review*, Jones is presented as working passionately 'from the real' in contrast to Pinero working decorously from fiction—in particular the fictitious world of Thackeray. Shaw, seems to have, built from this, his most imaginative literary device for matching their work.

Shaw's support of Jones, which he hoped would reveal a small fissure between smart society and the West End Theatre, involved much special pleading. Jones's plays, Shaw told his readers, were something disappointing because they were poorly performed by actors who had been taken out of routine parts and, for the first time in their careers, given something original, reflecting his own experience in 1897 with *You Never Can Tell.* Shaw opined that Jones's heroines were apt to die of nothing but the need for making the audience cry; he recognised the tendency of his last scenes to collapse, and his characters to act as if hypnotised by public opinion. But there was, as is apparent, a detachment in Jones when he portrayed Mayfair as an English traveler describing the Pygmies—that Shaw laboured to encourage. Shaw's statement about the towering height of English literature above English drama seems justified since literature is subject to no judgement but that of its natural masters (Holroyd: 335–339). Shaw, being the zeal of a literati, had, then, no problem to reshape the materials for the creation of something new. His characters could easily attain the level of credible familiarity: nubile maiden, idealist hero, stern parents; but their behaviour is unexpected. The consciousness of the Shavian heroines about their own romantic charm take the initiative in love-scenes and finally seduces the hero into accepting profit of slum landlordism. On the other hand, a Shavian idealist hero cannot bring himself to surrender his income merely for his ideals and, in the end, willingly succumbs to the heroines 'far from-moral suasion'. This deliberate reshaping, as it appears, not only gives birth to the flight from history in his earlier historical drama but also in the final-period creations like *Geneva*. In this play, every sensitive individual can sense, an increasing measure of agreement with the verdict of the Judge on Shaw's part. It describes an imaginary international court—scene in *Geneva*, presided over by the Dutch Judge and attended by caricatures of Mussolini, Hitler and Franco, together with other representatives of the conflicting ideologies of the twentieth century. They were all unanimous over the issue of Man's failure as a political animal. This is more a Shavian inference as we all know than the opinion of the delegates who attended the court in *Geneva*. There is an impression, too, in the late plays of a growing skepticism about the responsibility of bridging the dangerous gulf between enlightened intelligence and the centre of power (Gibbs: 36-37). So the play can better come under the category of literary creation than a history in the genre of William Shakespeare's. His was the natural rather than conventional history. Shaw tries to find out his dramas on what he regards as genuinely scientific natural history and since nothing can be more alien to scientific history than romance, Shaw's dramas are almost entirely devoid of sentiment. Probably, this is one of the qualities which distinguishes his plays not only with the dramas of a 'genuine romanticist' (Sengupta: 6-7) like William Shakespeare, but also from those of his own masters, Ibsen and Strindberg. None of his men speaks with the passion of a Gustar, nor have his women the deep emotional fervour of a Nora or a Mrs. Alivin. In his study of the world, Shaw has discovered that sentiment is always centered on the wrong thing.

Husbands are loved by their wives, though they are nothing but slave dealers; warriors are adored for their bravery, though the gallant V.C. very often lacks the courage to check a temptation that does not move a first-rate coward. Shaw, perhaps is not opposed to genuine emotion, as we can witness in the heroes of his historical plays, but before there can be any real sentiment we must be sure of the things about which these emotions are to be aroused. In his history plays the Shavian heroes are all first-rate people and hence their elementary feeling are all genuine. In general life, according to Shaw, most of our sentiments are based on poverty and inequality, which are the poisons that poses to destroy our civilisation. As long as this civilisation lasts, there can only be disease, sham sentiment and this sentimentality Shaw has rejected as unworthy of serious consideration.

Setting of Dramatic Form

As a playwright, as is generally acknowledged, Shaw wrote in the tradition of Moliere—a French writer of comedies and his business as a classic writer of comedies was to chasten morals with ridicules. Comedy as a form, as we all know, began with the satyr play following the tragic trilogy: in effect it was a mockery of the splendidly hideous events the spectators had just witnessed. Comedy was from the start derivative, secondary and purposively ignoble. Therefore, while a tragedy makes each member of an audience feel more distinguished than usual, a comedy encourages people to feel cheerfully mediocre. The first attitude may be described as a *pathos of separation* of oneself from others and the second as a *pathos of union*. Comedy, therefore, places the individual spectator back in the crowd, or keeps him there. He is varified as a bumbler or a comic rogue, a being of low value. In a comedy, as is natural, we are all poorish specimens and our decency lies in modestly recognising the fact.

Contrariwise, comedy keeps us in the realm of social reality and for practical purposes assumes that no character other than a social standard, which must inevitably lean towards the *democratic*. In the comic sphere we see with Rosencrantz and Guildenstern not Hamlet, and Hamlet's splendour becomes a pose or at most a reputation. He is obviously no more virtuous than we are, since we have never killed anyone or forced our fiancees to commit suicide. The fact that Hamlet is measuring us—mankind as a whole—by grander criteria never occurs to us. In any event such a grand way would simply be *his* way, his peculiarity, of no more value than our own idiosyncracies.

The chief attraction of a comedy for the audience, perhaps, is the opportunity to look down on most of the dramatis personae. If someone on the stage is witty than someone else in the play or far afield is the butt of his wit. As a rule we are taken up not so much with the skill of the epigram as with the inferiority of the victim. Our laughter is a wounding, even a negating of the victim. Therefore, comedy removes our cures by making us assume that nothing in the world—not sickness or death or dreamful crime—is actually serious. 'Ugliness is funny, accidents are funny, every sort of sorrow is a joke' (Keith: 207). The very people we find formidable in life are, it seems, ridiculous. Everything is absurd, so that all our fears and constraints flow away. There is nothing to be afraid of—but, at the same time, there is nothing to respect. In romantic comedy even the serious lovers are scarcely worthy of respect, for everyone is part of the comic totality.

Ibsen, perhaps alone in modern times, is properly apprehended as one who yearned to share the original Greek vision. He scarcely had a passionate delight in life in Kitto's sense but he wished he had and knew that the post Renaissance desire for change in society had weakened delight to the level of dreary pleasure. A similar accusation is levelled at Christianity in *Emperor and Galilean*. Shaw, on the other hand, believed altering society to be a source of delight in two senses: first, a revolutionists occupation might well be pleasurable in itself, and secondly, a new society should by definition contain fewer obstacle to happiness. More than that, Shaw's comedies aimed ultimately at changing not society alone but the biological foundation of human life. He assumed that natural conditions, as experienced by us, depend upon our opinions. Opinion, therefore, is the basis of every experience, for experiences, after earliest infancy, are always laden with value. Opinion is also the root from which God will develop, since we have the ability to create God ultimately out of our own convictions. Many people implicitly think the same, though they might be disturbed to see their assumption baldly stated.

Shaw, therefore, used comely to change opinion. But he was such a dialectician that whenever he saw a faulty notion he assumed that its opposite must be currect. The opposite of a fallacy is not merely a verity but *the* verity, so far as the dialectical mind can descern at any given moment. Thus, if longing for revenge is a psychological straitjacket imposed by romantic fiction, as it is in *Captain Brassbound's Conversation*, then all one has to do is to stop seeking revenge. A smart society may not, therefore, be dominated by general rule and a moralistic prescription for happiness.

The Shavian comic position was that the human will alone can undo the errors of the intellect, *which are errors of defeated will*. Perhaps they are, but Shaw never even glimpsed the true tragic position to the effect that the will must always be exercised and fairly regularly defeated. In this, far from being alone among comic authors, he was continuing the age-old comic tradition which conceived of defeat as humiliation. Next time, or at any rate some day, things will be different. As a rule Shaw himself seems anything but helpless. His comedy is knocking down of the old in order to build the new. Shaw like the Dorian revellers, rendered tragic action absurd and so turned pain into pleasure. Instead of seeing the natural joy in the pains of tragedy he found only misery, masked by idealism.

After the First World War, it was apparently imposible for new comers to write comedy of the hopeful Shavian sort. To the extent that later comedy has been of a new kind and it has seemed to be precisely hopeless. Perhaps the most revealing instance of this fresh tendency is the forerunner of all the rest; not a play but a story published as early as 1915, namely Kafka's *The Metamorphosis*. Gregor Samsa, having become a bug overnight, is comic because of the inadequacy of his response to his fate. In terms of values *The Metamorphosis* is at the farthest point from heroic poetry and tragedy. It also exhibits the one constant feature of later comic development.

For notable comedy has become almost exclusively absurdist, which is as much as to say, derived from Kafka. It is important to grasp the metaphysical implications of such works, or rather, the absence of metaphysics which the authors are comically lamenting. Absurd drama is not a set of techniques but a fretting, an anger, a harsh mockery about the vanity of our lives. But we have brought about the vanity by abandoning divine values yet not replacing them with personal judgments of the same hierarchical and discriminatory kind. To put the matter another way, in the eyes of the Church all are equally loved but not all are equally good. Some deeds are certainly worthier than others. The new secular attitude is to the effect that no deed is necessarily worthier than another, except, of course, that discrimination itself is deplorable.

The main line of Shaw's development might be loosely summed up as a movement from naturalism to distinctive forms of comic and tragic—comic fantasy. In comedy there is not much room and little occasion for profound character analysis. In choosing the lighter genres of drama, Shaw wisely avoided the intricacies of a type of introspection for which he had no taste, and possibly not much aptitude. If we agree that Shaw's plays are fabulistic it must be granted that they have all the reality of fables, and it is not reasonable to require more of the fabulist than the measure of reality a fable can accommodate. The setting of many of his works of the early and middle period—in hotels, drawing rooms, studies and offices and the like—lend some semblance of a solid basis in familiar reality. Character portrayal in the plays before *Back to Methuselah* is usually fairly detailed in its attention to individual distinguishing features of personality, and an air of reliability is added by the fact that Shaw so often cuts through patterns of feeling suggested by fictional conventions to a substratum of more plausible motive and impulses. But even in this period Shaw's playful comic imagination continually takes us beyond the confines of naturalistic convention. In his first two plays, namely *Widower's House* and *The Philanderer,* mere facts of life are treated with a colouring of extravagant satirical comedy. In the comedy of *The Philanderer,* especially that surrounding the manly sentiments of the theatre critic Cuthbertson, and the failure of Dr. Paramore's medical theory, Shaw laid the foundations of a style which was to be characteristic of the plays of his early and middle periods, and for which the phrase *fantastic fidelity* seems appropriate. More complete departures from naturalism in the late period are anticipated in such scenes as Caesar's address to the Sphinx in *Caesar and Cleopetra,* the Dream Sequence in *Man and Superman* and in most of the actions in *Androcles and the Lion.* Shaw's *The Devil's Disciple* narrates the story of American War of Independence. The scene is located in new Hampshire, then a wilderness of forests and mountains, through which Burgoyne leads his army to Boston, and from that city down to Hudson to Albany. As well might Shaw, in stating a French invasion of England, have portrayed the enemy as marching around the English channel to Glasgow and down the Clyde to London. Burgoyne's tyranny is ultimately nulified by the stage tricks of Dick. It is the stage tricks and clever dialogues through which Shaw made his play thrilling by banishing the tragic strain.

Quite often Shaw produced laughter with the help of paradox. It is apparent in his style, and is just as marked in his characterisation. Mrs. Warren, for instance, far from being a monster or a fallen woman with a heart of gold, is engagingly poor. The success of *Pygmalion* depends largely on the failure of Doolittle to live up to the conventional image of a dustman. In his very first play, *Widower's House*, Shaw showed us a transformation scene when the downtrodden rent collector, Lickcheese, reappeared in the last act splendidly dressed as a successful businessman. Something of the same kind happens in *Pygmalion* when Doolittle appeared resplendently dressed as for a formal wedding. Higgins's joke of recommending the dustman to an American millionaire as the original moralist of the recent time in England has caused him to be conditionally left with 4,000 pounds a year in the millionaire's will. The idea is of course, preposterous, but Shaw makes serious use of it, as well as giving us plenty to laugh about in Doolittle's panic-stricken reaction to his unwanted respectability.

To create comic atmosphere, Shaw did not hesitate to cut anti-English jokes. In *Caesar and Cleopatra,* Shaw had deliberately gone out of his way to create an anachronistic ancient Briton to act as secretary-companion to Caesar. The portrayal of the character of Britannus was theatrically effective. His self-assessed righteousness on every occasion relieves with comic effect. Similarly Napoleon's long speech about the English in *The Man of Destiny*, and in de Stogumber's ridiculous attitude in *Saint Joan*, Shaw is in his most impish vein. He realised, as Shakespeare did before him, that the audience is flattered when it is most insulted. We have only to remember the grave-digger's exchange with Hamlet to see the truth of this observation.

In major history plays also, domination of comic strain is maintained throughout. In *The Man of Destiny*, the situations—such as the loss of the despatches, the discovery of the strange lady by the Lieutenant, the struggle between the man of destiny and the lady—appear to have created a dramatic illusion to strengthen a temporary suspension of disbelief. The stage trick of suspense is maintained properly and throughout, perhaps, to ensure a typical Shavian comic environment.

In *Caesar and Cleopatra*, Shaw could keep his comic vision intact, by attributing everlastingness to certain earthly qualities like womanly beauty and charm. From syntactical point of view his poerty becomes one with his vision. The domination of laughing-whisper and the clever dialogue orientation enhnaces the nuancy of comic spirit.

Shaw's famous religious historical play *Saint Joan* achieves a unique and almost perfect integration of high comic power with strong conviction. The tragedy of Joan's murder is that it is not committed by murderers. Shaw preferred to level it as a judicial murder or a pious murder. This contradiction at once brings an element of comedy into the tragedy: the angels may weep at the murder, but the Gods laugh at the murderers (Preface to *Saint Joan*: 631). According to Christain theology, Joan's journey leads her towards absolute happiness, and thus converting herself almost to a Christ figure. The scenes and act, from where the action of the play begins laughter has been knitted with comedy (e.g., three Barbbary hens and black).

In Good King Charles's Golden Days is a scintillating comedy, written when Shaw was eighty-three years old. The play has no plot, and the characters generally express opinions on various problems from Shavian point of view. The play is divided into two acts and in the first act Shaw assembles all the four protagonists and mainly the mistresses of Charlse-II in Isaac Newton's house at Cambridge. The unending dialogues of the protagonists is highly intellectual, and it is difficult to maintain mental allertness at so long a stretch. In lesser hands the long discussion would have flagged. But the adoption of comic devices by Shaw made the discussion extremely lively, exhilarating and captivating. The sense of reconciliation and hearty conversation between Charlse-II and queen Catherine in act-II is, perhaps, intentded to provide us with a comic relief.

Shaw's laughter, as may be safely affirmed, is primarily rooted in his ideas. For an example—Mr. Alfred Doolittle, father of the flower- girl Eliza in *Pygmalion,* a play ostensibly on the subject of phonetics with its own implications. Doolittle has nothing to do with the subject of the play, but he has a philosophy of his own, which puts to shame both capitalism and socialism. Capitalism believes in free enterprise which will enable a man to earn by virtue of his abilities and then contribute to the state and also to benevolent organisations. But as his name implies, Eliza's father can do nothing and make no contribution to the state revenues. Socialism, on the other hand, believes in distributing the gross national income according to a man's need. Doolittle earns nothing, but his needs are very large, because he eats a lot and drinks a lot more. A righteous widow will attract the attention of charitable institutions, but what about him and what will the socialist state take from a man who is temperamentally unfit to work?

Shaw is a comedian because he has a genius for raising laughter, but he is a great comedian, because his laughter is inspired by lofty ideas, by hatred of cruelty and love of life.

Socialistic Perspective

The genesis of the Shavian History Plays, may be considered to vindicate the two principal socio-political problems which disturbed him much. The causes were related to the problem of finding a proper ruler where the ruler's stamp is not misutilised and the problem of equal distribution of wealth to ensure a smooth and classless society. Practically the latter leads him towards the Fabianist group of social reformers which had many things to do with the conception of Marxism. Shaw's theory of value was, as was Karl Marx's, the hub of an analysis of capitalism. And this may also be taken to mean not only that Shaw's economic essays are infinitely smaller things in intention and effect than Marx's but that Shaw is much less of a believer in static laws both in economics and nature. He seized on Jevons because the latter seemed to leave a loophole for human will and effort. In Jevons, there was no law of motion of capitalism, no historical inevitability. Shaw fought the Marxists whenever, as it appears, like the Darwinists, they seemed to be determinists.

The discussion of value was opened and closed in the eighties. The matter of class-struggle needed a lengthier airing. Once again Shaw's chief antagonist was the contemporary English champion of Marx, H.M. Hyndman. Shaw's argument in this battle was not in the least the argument of classical economy—that there is a harmony of interest between capital and labour. He fully agreed with Marx that there was no such harmony operating in the society. He did not agree, however, that present antagonisms of interest would automatically induce the proletariat to struggle for power. Again, it is the law of history, the historical necessity, the inevitability, that Shaw objects to. He fears that reliance on them is as futile as reliance on God and that to wait for history to produce socialism is to wait for ever. When the Marxist replies to that if the workers are not class-conscious they must be made so, he is, of course appealing from historical necessity to the will of a minority. Shaw is not averse to this. He merely concludes that so prompted the struggle for socialism will have lower and upper class people on both sides and is, therefore, not accurately described as a class struggle.

The Fabians fail to see the historic mission of the working class. For the Fabians deny that such things as historic mission exists. And it is true—they are unique as post-Marxists socialist in putting on no more faith in the proletariat as such than in any other group. Shaw has always held that if the poor were already wiser and better than anybody else that would be a reason for keeping them poor. His socialism resembles to that of D.H. Lawrence in that he wishes to do nothing with the proletariat except abolish it. At this point, the Marxist abandons his argument of necessity and appeals to pure sentiment, to that praise of the poor as poor which is the essence of demagogy. Theoretically, the Marxist should not believe in the superiority of the poor or in the villainy of the rich. Actually very much Marxist propaganda does posit these things. The Fabians offered a much less dramatic programme: that of permeating the liberals, of using parliamentary methods, of gradualness. The defense of the Fabian position is two-fold. First, sanity is often less exciting than insanity second, permeation and gradualness were the beginning, not the end, of Fabian policy. That the Fabian policy was sane is shown by the astonishing measure of success which attended it. No group of philosophers since the Benthamites had conceived so well how to get the optimum result. It would be impossible to account for the social legislation of England in the twentieth century without the work of preparation performed by such people as the Webbs. But nobody should think that the matter of show-down and violence, it was Shaw who led, and the Webbs came to the Shavian conclusion much later. Same was the situation with the question of leadership. The Webbs had, as is conceived, always believed in the expert but they had imagined him wholly as servant and not a leader. Shaw, as is clear, did not leave it to Lenin or Stalin to give him a belief in the active leader who does much more than merely carry out the expressed will of the masses. One need hardly cite his *Caesar and Cleopatra*, his prefatorial praise of the Bismarkian man of action who will sweep away all humbug, or his doctrine of Superman. The most acute analyst of Shaw's socialism in the early days, Max Beer, saw in it all the things that would later offend the Liberals.

Writing in 1904 from the Marxist point of view, Max Beer stamped Shaw as a victim of relativism. In his opinion, probably, finding no objective guide, no leading principle to go by, Shaw necessarily arrives at hero-worship—at the hankering after a Superman to guide mankind. Beer noticed the same mental development, as was in Shaw, in several continental critics like Harden, Bahr, Ernst etc. In his opinion, they all began with Social Democracy, passed through the Ibsen period, worshipped *An Enemy of the People*, finally becoming adherents of Nietzsche in theory and of Bismarck or other social imperialist in practice. Marxism is the antithesis of all that. In his conception it has a body of doctrines; it regards theory as the guide in practical life; and it destroys all heroism in history. In the place of the heroic factor it sets material and economic factors as the motor power of historical development. To the Revisionists or Fabians, socialism, as had been defined by them, is not a class struggle, but a clever management of public affair. It is the Superman in local government.

Most of Beer's assertions have a solid foundation. But it is hard to agree with the point to consider the statement: 'socialism is...the Superman in local government', because the very conception of Superman totally denies the basic socialistic ideal of governing force emerging from the common mass. In strict communist terms this is ineffably bourgeois conception—that a power from outside will come to rescue worldly people from all socio-politico-economic problems. This, in other way, is denying the communist conception of collective potentiality in human beings. It is comparable to a communist's dream for a super-bourgeois force. But in that social perspective it was not unnatural. When the conception of neo-communism started shaping its model, the learned class thought that a messianic force has come to save people from the chaotic situation. But when the theory came into practice, the leader remained the same with their shaven face, it resulted in a great fiasco (New York Herald, 1925). So, naturally, the political thinkers lost their faith and conscious people started thinking of something new. Shaw, accordingly, rooted his faith in the conception of Superman. He rearranged historical facts and characters to show some traits of Superman in them. And to give enough credibility, he took up the historical personages respect for whom is automatically guaranteed. His historical characters such as Napoleon, Joan, Charles all got his force and created a history of its own genre.

Shaw was anti-authoritarian in communism, as well as in his idea of the word 'history'. One may assume that *Caesar and Cleopatra* is a melodrama and one of the three plays for Puritans. It is also the second of the four history plays—*The Man of Destiny, Saint Joan* and *In Good King Charles's Golden Days* are the other three—in which Shaw worked at his problem by connecting it with great historical figures. One must, however, be very clear about the fact that Shaw had never been interested to perform the job of a professional historian. As his way had been, he informed everybody that his plays were utterly historical and defended their most whimsical anachronisms in notes. However, there were scholars who felt for it and earnestly corrected Shaw's facts in solemn articles.

Shaw, on the other hand, defended his point by telling that he learnt history by intuition. He wrote his plays first and read the history books afterwards, and found, as he said, that he was right all along, in giving Caesar and a certain set of circumstances a replica of what would have happened to them. Those who think this a naive confession are themselves naïve. Many would prefer the fictional biographies of Shavian history plays which,—though based on deep research and understanding, every fact guaranteed—are humanly absurd as was Kitsch in Metro—Goldwyn—Mayer settings designed by historical research. Shaw's method is rather opposite, he prefers to retain his right to be absurd in everything but psychology. He recognised a limitation in all objective historical writing, and thus led to believe that our understanding of an historical character is a highly subjective affair. What Shaw confessed his personal shortcoming is a general human one: 'As a dramatist I have no club to any historical or other personage save that part of him which is also myself...that can ever come within my knowledge of his soul'.

Shaw differs from a sound historian not only in being more subjective but also in not being a historian at all in the traditional sense of the term. In his history plays Shaw was, as is evident, not interested in the peculiar character of each period—Napoleonic, ancient or medieval—but in indicating what has not changed, particularly, in psychological similarity of character through the ages. Seeing and hearing people much alike ourselves the audience learns that no progress has been made during historical time. This being the case, themes and settings are part of the game Shaw plays with his audience; as regard technique, they are a parody of the Lyceum and other period pieces. Just as in *You Never Can Tell* he boasts of giving the gallery all it wants by the way of good wine and carnival dresses, so he might boast of the good time he gives his audiences with his historical costumes. Apollodorus's flight to the Pharo's he calls a prodigious harlequin leap.

Probably another purpose Shaw had in choosing historical characters for his plays about power is that such characters have a mysterious authority. Napoleon, Caesar and Joan existed in real life. The audience, therefore, feels them to be real and tangible. Here it may be acknowledged, safely, that a famous historical personage can often be termed 'legendary'. Shaw chooses only those legendary names from the pages of history. And his plays have much more loyalty to the legend than to the fact. Just as the whole show is something of a parody of the Kitsch costume play, the character of the hero is always a variant—never a debunking—of the popular legend: the granite-faced Caesar, Napoleon as he appears in David's portraits, Joan as interpreted by Schiller or Mark Twain.

For those who understand the drift of Shaw's history plays the controversies over the facts in *Saint Joan* are not relevant. Aside from Quicherat, it seems that all Shaw read about Joan of Arc were the plays and biographies that had helped to create her legend—or rather her legends, for Joan is every sort of villain or heroine to every sort of sect. Shaw can not see her—can not see anybody, least of all a genius—as either villain or heroine. Nor can he allow her judges to be assigned the opposite role—villains if she is a heroine, heroes if she is a villain. To Shaw, as is evident, the versions of Joan of Arch provided by William Shakespeare, Schiller, Mark Twain and the rest are all melodramatic variations on an impossible theme. They see the characters as morally one-sided and the conclusion of Joan's story as a simple phenomenon: simply pathetic, simply glorious, simply atrocious, simply a good thing or simply a bad thing. These legends appear to have not satisfied Shaw, who began rejecting villains and heroes. He must show, as is natural in a Shavian play, Joan as a credible human being and unlike most of her humanizing biographers, Shaw must make her greatness credible. As for the vast forces which crushed her, since they are of human creation, he must make them credible too. If Joan's judges were really cheap politicians then her story had best be left alone as a cheap story. If there is a drama in it, it lies in the collision of the two forces, both profoundly human, both eminently defensible, both, perhaps, necessary.

A G.B. Shaw play is, from its aim and impression, about the individual and the collective or—if we think of it in terms of time—the simultaneous need for stability and change. Shaw is not one with the anarchists and their myriad unconscious sympathisers, he resents authority; he finds it requisite for order and permanence. He cannot, with the authoritarian reject non-conformity; he finds it requisite for all human development.

Evolutionary Perspective

The unique treatment of historical materials by Shaw appears to be deeply rooted in his being a, self-fashioned, Creative Evolutionist. From the dramatic point of view, however, it is the poetic side of Shaw's theology that is also interesting. In the theatre, his idea of Life Force seems magnificently fruitful. It provided a theoretical basis for conflict which exalts drama far above the monotonous struggle of good and evil, and it provides a teleological framework for situations which in present state of faith, quite defy resolution. The fact that this teleology is wholly conjectural can hardly trouble those for whom reality has, in any case, become increasingly a matter of conjecture. What Shaw provided was, probably, a dramatic system which has enormous possibilities if one is willing to grant its assumptions. On the other hand, if one is not willing to grant the same it appears to be sufficiently logical within its framework to support the necessary illusion. In a period when much of English drama consisted of miniature transactions which scarcely repay the effort of attention, in Shaw's plays, on the other hand, the canvas is so vast as to encompass the whole reach of human destiny. Not all of Shaw's drama, of course, does so much. But of the two-score plays that have come from his 'shop', atleast a half dozen must be accounted for the first importance. With the exception of William Shakespeare, not so much can be said of any English dramatist.

Shaw appears to have taken enough time to attain this order of greatness. At that time he was writing *The Man of Destiny* he was still at some way from forming a general idea. Even after he found his certainty, much more was needed to frame a work of art of the very first order. The Hegelian idea of history suggested a useful method for the dramatic confrontation of conflicting ideas. But it is universally acknowledged that art is a sublimation of thought, not thought itself. The Greek tragedies had been written in the light of the Homeric world-view; Shakespeare had framed his drama within the cosmic outlines of Renaissance Christianity. History of literature tells us that neither Sophocles nor Shakespeare needed to define the cosmic ambience in which their plays took place, but by 1895 the intellectual horizon had widened beyond the reach of man's vision, and the exact positioning of the Renaissance artist had dwindled into nothing. Shaw's drama, as is hypothesised, had to be provided with a cosmic frame based on philosophic concepts which must be defined and justified in the course of the action. The necessary exposition could well be relegated to the reading matter appended to the play; but on the stage the invisible must be suggested through symbols. Before a work of art of very first rate could be achieved in the ordinary way of the theatre, the symbols had to be found, and also the symbolism. (Valency: 406-407).

As regards the spirit, Shaw was an ardent worshipper of the creed of Creative Evolution. Naturally, he considered everyone as an experiment of the Life Force. He looked into the pages of history to search out the really great man who can be viewed as an exponent of the force. He had a purpose to set example of great historical figures, like Napoleon, Caesar, Saint Joan, whose evolutionary qualities may remain as an ideal which the coming generation might admire and imitate in their practical life. In each of his historical plays, Shaw kept his attention riveted on a great individual, an individual of central historical significance. His purpose was to bring out the heroic qualities of the individuals and he often brought them out quite successfully. But he often tailored his hero to his own particular vision of greatness. A clear conception of the Shavian vision of greatness is, thus, a prerequisite for proper understanding of his historical plays.

A great man, in the Shavain vision, is a man of originality and this originality, perhaps, gives him 'an air of frankness, generosity and magnanimity by enabling him to estimate the value of truth, money or success in any particular instance quite independently of convention and moral generation'. He is a realist and hence free from romantic illusion and sees things exactly as they are. A great experiment of the Life Force, a great man has, above all, an indomitable will. He, always, wills to do good for the earth and the earthly. In finer analysis, this appears to be the purpose of the Almighty. Hence, a great man, in the Shavian sense, symbolises, in his own way, a miniature God and is very much relevant in any practical situation. It appears that he has his eyes fixed on his goal from which he will never turn aside and for which all causes must give way. To reach his goal, as we can conceive, he may act with entire selfishness, tell dexterous lies and stoop to any kind of subterfuge. All these qualities endow a Shavian great man with rare personality and power which, the people around him, would feel. He can therefore, manipulate things and beings to suit his own purpose. In a subtler analysis, it assumes that the purpose, ultimately, is not his own but of Nature's. He, as it appears, becomes an instrument through which Nature performs her tasks. But in this process his intellect is never beglamoured or his aim shaken by a sense of his own power or by any other passion, particularly never by love of women. The love of women at best can refine his sentiment but can not deviate him from his chosen path. He is conscious of his great purpose and he possesses the will to act upon it. This high degree of will accounts for his tremendous control over himself. A Shavian great man is not free from fear, and he, also, appears to be without courage which is a prime virtue of Carlyle's and Nietzsche's heroes. But he wills his end so strongly that even the one universal passion, fear finds no place in him. And though without courage, his mind is so firmly fixed on his goal that he ignores all dangers. Thus, as we can think, he flies in the face of danger not because he possesses courage in the sense of a disposition to defy danger but because he is oblivious of it. Shaw's Napoleon, for example, knows 'fear well, better than you, better then any woman', but once on the bridge at Lodi it cannot hold him back. Oblivious of fear, a greatman is also oblivious of courage. Eric Bentley, aptly opines: 'if Nietzsche's hero is beyond good and evil Shaw's is beyond courage and cowardice' (170).

In the Shavian postulation, a great man triumphs over his environment and achieves his goal by virtue of his intelligence and shrewdness, goal by virtue of his intelligence and shrewdness, but more by his unconventional attitude and steady will power. He is, in the Shavian assumption, not the creature of his age but its creator, not its servant but its master. He controls events and drives society in his intended direction. This is a genius which means clear sightedness, will and ability to influence other people. This conception of the great man brings Shaw into sharp conflict with the scientific view of history. A scientific historian, as we all know, seeks to explain all changes in thought, all movements in politics and society in terms of unswerving natural laws. The individual, according to this view, is immersed in and driven by the current of social tendencies. The scientific historian looks upon social life as an organism unfolding in Shavian belief, is inevitable, because man has the power to control itself according to immanent laws; either of racial individuality or of a combination of social, physical and personal forces. The spirit of a people and of an age outweighs the power of an individual's personality which can work only along socially conditioned tendencies. The habit of a scientific historian is, thus, to subordinate, if not quite eliminate, the individual; the great man is treated by him as in a large measure the product and expression of the spirit of time. For Shaw, on the other hand, the great man is supreme. External circumstances and influences count little. The root of the Shavian over-dependence on the conception of great man may, also, be traced in his growing dissatisfaction with the progress of human beings as a race. It is apparent that his Irish sensibility, unlike an Englander, made him dependent on the 'natural freak' for breaking the stagnation of human progress. Shaw believed that human beings—the descendant of Yahoo—are in need of a good leader for proper guidance. Greatmen gave him something to look forward to, something to hope for. The Shavian conception, thus, permeates the greatman to surmount the environmental forces and it is his personal initiative that accounts for history. Thus, Shaw like Carlyle, is the pioneer of a historical literature.

The Shavian vision of history, appears to be, very opposite to deterministic. The determinists conceptualise history as the record of a constant process of evolution towards a predetermined goal in which a great man plays only a very limited part while Shaw regards the course of history as flexible and open to salutary modification by the well instructed human will. The idea of human will looms large in the Shavian vision of history.

Anti-scientific in his reading of history, Shaw is also, as it appears to be, anti-democratic in the lesson he deduces from it. Each of his history plays is the product of a great mind in opposition to the rabble. Shaw laments that there has been no progress during the last two and a half thousands years, but he believes in the possibility of progress. History gives glimpse of progress followed by decadent civilisations. Occasional progress has been possible only because of superior individuals who had the greatness to bring order out of chaos and turn decadence to discipline. But greatmen are rare and, therefore, there has been no continuity of progress. This idea seems implicit behind the conception of the Shavian histories. The lesson that can be derived from these play is, perhaps, that the one hope of the distracted world lies in the strength and wisdom of the few, not in the original unwisdom of the many. The masses of people, in the Shavian assumption, can never solve for themselves, the intricate problems of their own welfare. They need to be guided, disciplined, at times, even driven, by those great leaders of men who know much better than they can ever know what is good for them, and how that good is to be attained. In the preface to *Back to Methuselah,* Shaw wrote in 1920 of a doubt which had grown steadily in his mind during his fifty years public work as a socialist, whether 'the human animal...is capable of solving the social problems raised by his own aggregation or, as he calls it, his civilization' (502). And earlier, in 1901, in *The Revolutionist Handbook* he had already reiterated the need for the superman. Shaw, to conclude the present discussion, like Carlyle, appears to be anti-scientific and anti-democratic in his study of history. It may be safely affirmed, in this context, that Shaw worshipped the Clio, after placing her at the alter of Creative Evolution.

NOTE

1. Throughout Shaw's career in office he kept up an almost daily letter-writing duel with an old school-boy companion named Edward McNulty, later the author of three novels about Irish life. Their letters, which were of a highly romantic order, were illustrated with crude drawing and enlivened by burlesque dramas. This outlet for his intellectual activities was very attractive to him and it also worked off his incipient literary energy. They have agreed to destroy the letters and none seems to have survived.

3 Estimation of Select History Plays

THE MAN OF DESTINY

The Man of Destiny is the first of the historical plays of Shaw. It has been projected as an entertaining play and seems to be far away from the historical veracity. In its first appearance, the dramatic probability of the play was wrongly criticised. *The Man of Destiny*, is seen less as a play than a simple medium for airing Shavian vision about socialism, political economy, the aggrandisement of England and other cognate matters. The critics further, commonly postulated that discussion on a piece of that kind would be a waste of time and space. They, however, did not deny the real cleverness to be found in the dialogues but they opined it to be a kind of cleverness 'ill-suited to the purpose of the stage' (Nicoll: 204).

The validity of such comment appears to be faulty enough so far as its artistic quality is concerned. In the Preface to *Plays Pleasant* Shaw described it as 'a bravura piece' (Shaw: 730), to display the 'virtuosity' (Ibid: 730), of the two main actors. In course of progress of the play, artistic aim being the principal guideline, Shaw appears to have faced no problem in negating the proper spirit of the Clio for inviting a romantic mood favourable to the stage of the day. The loss of the despatches, the discovery of the Strange Lady by the Lieutenant, the struggle between the man of destiny and the lady—all these appear to have created a dramatic illusion to strengthen a temporary suspension of disbelief. The stage trick of suspense is maintained throughout the entire course of the play. In case of dramatisation of a historical play, it is generally believed that a dramatist has to perform this task if there is a conscious departure from the world of facts.

The story material, also, tells about a romantic story dealing in a probability—what could have been. Naturally, it describes a small fictitious incident of Napoleon's life on 12 May, 1796, when he was still a general commanding the army of Italy. There is a strange encounter with a strange lady in the inn where he sojourns. The total episode of the letter and the encounter between Napoleon and the Strange Lady are pieces in Shavian creation. Josephine was the former mistress of Barras, one of the Directors. Nepoleon married her on 9 March, 1796, and parted after two days to command the army of Italy. Shaw imagines that during Napoleon's absence one of the letters of Barras to Josephine got mixed up with the official despatches. Shaw, probably, stresses Napoleon's exceptional endowments and masterful will-power to imply the *sine-qua-non* of a Shavian greateman.

The wave of fiction continues to grab the story, up to the moment, when some despatches which Napoleon has been waiting for have been wheedled out of his lieutenant by a confident trick played by a lady disguised as an Austrian officer. By sheer accident the lady puts up in the inn where Napoleon is staying, a co-incident which makes Napoleon's task easy to ask about his despatches:

> 'You tricked that blockhead out of them. You disguised yourself as a man. I want my despatches. They are there in the bosom of your dress, under your hands' (370–373). There ensues a struggle for the letters. To achieve her end she proves to be no less formidable a rival to Napoleon than a Wellington or a Pitt. The entire episode is designed, as it appears, to portray a war of wills between the two. It is not so much Napoleon's purpose and will as his original outlook on life and the world that Shaw lays emphasis on. He, perhaps, performs the task either of a philosopher or a psychologist—but in no way the task of a historian. His flight from the history towards an unconventional world is even more clear when Shaw passed his opinion that Napoleon's superiority lies in his possession of original values, in his immunity from conventional codes of conduct. In this process, *The Man of Destiny* becomes an inner story

> of a conflict between realism and idealism, between an unconventional outlook and the accepted code of conjugal fidelity. This, perhaps, qualifies Shaw's Napoleon to become a masterful realist, unhampered by any altruism or any conventional code of morality.

Aristotle might have thought that the principal concern of the dramatist is drama. But Shaw, as it appears, considered that the main business of the dramatist is to tell the underlying truth. In the Shavian postulation, every conscious dramatist is a conscious philosopher. He does not create illusions; he makes men disillusioned. He is a keen observer and a serious thinker, concerned primarily with reality, and reality is what is perceived when the essential design of things becomes visible. A work of art based on such premises will be, above all, meaningful, and the result in an aesthetic experience found on comprehension. The pleasure of the theatre, as is clear, becomes the pleasure of understanding. Shaw's Napoleon, therefore, although a realist does not respect the rules of war, yet he dignifies war with the noise and smoke of cannon, as depicted in all military portraits. As an original observer he ignores the old fashioned art of war, revolutionising warfare by developing the use of artillery in an unprecedented way.

Therefore, the Shavian calculation, probably, allowed the outlined story run in favour of waging a war of will to establish that Napoleon's rise to power was not as accident but of certain exceptional mental endowments. To achieve his goal, perhaps, Shaw used the technique of contrast. The romantic commander, who is duped to believe that the strange lady is the sister of the Austrain officer, which the conventional history may not approve, who robbed him of the despatches throws into relief Napoleon's foresightedness which can see through apparent haziness. The characteristic traits of the strange lady—such as the conventional indifference, altruism and her physical charm are meant to act, probably, as a foil to the man of destiny's original outlook and his capacity to control the 'strongest of all human passions'. Shaw's ways of testing a person's fixity to goal by treating him with sexual firmness have, as it seems, a correlation with Freudian concept of psycho-analysis, where 'libido' is considered to be the most powerful of all human passions. According to this concept, though a bit exaggerated, all human relations are mainly guided by sex instinct where even the complexes are believed to be natural. So it is apparent that Shaw has used the physical allurement of the strange lady to seduce the man of destiny—the temptation which Samson—the Miltonic hero could not overcome. But the Shavian Napoleon remains victorious in successfully conquering the physical allurement. In this process, Shaw could set before us one of the criteria for evaluating the Shavian greatman.

The happy journey from history is not an accident as is clear from Shaw's letter to Ellen Terry (Christopher: 143), where he acknowledges that *The Man of Destiny* display the Shavian knowledge of stage tricks. He appears to have been fully conscious of what the audience demanded, and he made use of certain elements that meant for popularity. Shaw, seems to be willing and eager to make full and free employment of physical action on the stage—'the eternally exciting appeal of melodrama'—and to utilise those conceptions which made the burlesque, 'the force and the extravaganza once so popular (Nicoll: 196)—about which the historical chronology is silent. This may account for the course and vigorous conversation between Napoleon and Giuseppe with which the play opens, the lieutenant's flamboyant speech beginning with 'Nothing happened to me!' (200), his over exciting speeches and actions to see the lady, Nepoleon's theatrical gestures, pose and action before her. One may feel that the man of destiny could get the despatches without making so much ado, but Shaw knew better, and he exploited the amoristic intrigue and the histrionics of the nineteenth century history play to produce greater theatrical effect and to capture the mind of the audience.

The Man of Destiny is an interesting play because of its two-way interpretations of becoming the first of the Shavian history play and secondly in the sketch of Napoleon the Shavian concept of greatness is revealed, though not with full prescription, for the first time. Shaw, here, is telling the story of a legendary, mythical, superhuman taking few traits of this historical character. Probably, to invest the Shavian treatment on this legend, Shaw had to allow fiction to supercede facts. It dose not sound unnatural to any student of Shaw as they already know that Shaw only wanted a great man from history on whom his own beliefs could easily be ascribed. So, probably, Shaw retells a story, in his own way, about a Napoleon who is off the battlefield and through a short and simple incident revealed the strength and weakness of his character.

It appears that Shaw tried to write of one universal passion: fear, particularly in his *The Man of Destiny.* It is to be noted here that, the play may be considered to have its origin in the haphazard story telling sequence between Shaw and the famous actress Ellen Terry. In 1895, when Shaw revealed in his one act play for Napoleon and a Strange Lady that their flirtatious correspondence really opened. It was, probably, this fear, as Michael Holroyd pointed out, that confined them to an invisible island of enchantment where there was no pain or regret and no growing old. They knew about them such things and, when the atmosphere of charm lifted a little, could spy them far off, even mimic them; then go back to their play—acting together (Holroyd: 348). This was the practice, his expression of humanitarian love for Ellen Terry in papers, and, probably, for this reason Shaw could not write for her one of his great plays but offered her instead this trifle, *The Man of Destiny*,—'a perfectly idiotic play' that itself revolved around a piece of paper, a supposed love letter. The historical accuracy of the episodes may also be disapproved if we analyse the Shavian estimation where he acknowledges that he has written this play out of the densest historical and geographical ignorance and his model for Napoleon was nobody but Richard Mansfield.

It may be safely postulated that there is a marked tendency in Shaw's Napoleon for making him a commonplace hero by attributing shabbiness and untidy table habits. This tendency is even more clear in the stage direction where Napoleon's elbow seems to have displaced most of the dishes and glasses; and his long hair into the risotto when he forgets it and leans more intently over the map. It appears that Shaw has brought the hero off his pedestal, but he has done so in deference to reality. He remains loyal to the Clio when he tells that Napoleon did not pay enough of attention to his person or dress. This statement gets support when John Holland Rose, after Napoleon's victory of Lody, tells '...gazed with admiration, not unmixed with awe, at the pale feature of the young commander whose plain attire bespoke a Spartan activity' (96). The Shavian description of Nepoleon has a similarity with the portraiture of Napoleon by Appiani in 1976. Shaw's description of Nepoleon, also runs in conformity with the comments of Wallace. K. Ferguson and Geoffrey Bruun when they personified him as the youthful general of twenty-seven who routed the Austrians in Italy was 'lean unkempt and shabby, but his sharp gaze could disconcert older and more experienced Officers' (624). Shaw appears to have found a solid biographical support when he tells of Napoleon's indifference to environment and physical appearance amply testifies to the tremendous power of his mind to concentrate on the immediate object of pursuit. But these are the mere facts Shaw, perhaps, takes to satisfy the popular theatre-goers for converting a popular hero into a Shavian philosopher. He appears to have found out a superman only from the pages of history—respect for whom was automatically guaranteed.

The greatest quality of the Shavian Napoleon, probably, is that he, ultimately, could prove himself to be above jealousy. Shaw expressed his opinion just after witnessing Madam—Sans—Gene of M.M. Sardou in Lyceum theatre on 10 April, 1896. He was, rather, dissatisfied with M.M. Sardou's Napoleon, whom he described as 'nothing but the Jealous Husband of a thousand fashionable drama's taking Buonapartiana (Shaw: 110). The Shavian man of destiny seems to be quite the opposite of the Jealous Husband. The lady, who is conventional to the core, is sure that the revelation in the letter would mean a duel with Barras resulting in a broken house hold and public scandal. Napoleon, as is understood, reads the letter secretly and gives it back to the lady pretending that he has not read it. He tries not to acknowledge it, probably, to ignore his wife's unchastity.

So much of intentional transformation and the denial of historical exactitude, in the beginning, had caused a great displeasure of his admirers. Mansfield contemptuously declined it. Augustin Hamon, Shaw's French translator, opined that Shaw had read 'all the wrong Books about the Emperor' (Ervine: 283). It is perceived later on that the problem had very little to do with the wrong books he went through, rather it can safely be categorised as Shavian way of interpretation and his individual estimation about this great man of history. Once again, Sir Henry Irving aired his opinion by telling that G.B Shaw had no respect for great man and distinguished people, and it must have seemed to him that the portrait of Napoleon in *The Man of Destiny* was blasphemous' [Ibid: 289]. Eric Bentley opines that Napoleon, here, is little more than a parody of 'L' Empereur, though a parody that should make the audience smile on the wrong side of its face. Since the hero's heroism is not really impugned, Shaw has made it clear that he means the piece as 'a theatrical exercise for virtuosi' (Bentley: 104). Gordon Craig opines that the stage business is a transcript of some of Henry Irving's favourite stage behaviour. If Napoleon is more than a puppet it is because Shaw tries to infuse into him something of himself as one would gather at least from the stage direction. Here he is projected as a man with prodigious power of work, and a clear realistic knowledge of human nature in public affairs. Again, he is, as is apparent, imaginative without illusions, and creative without religion, loyalty, patriotism or of the common ideals. He is not paying any heed to the ideals, probably, as he had swallowed them all in his boyhood, and, now, having a keen dramatic faculty, is extremely clever at playing upon them by the arts of the actor and stage manager. It is apparent that neither he is a spoiled child nor he had been struck by poverty, ill-luck, the shifts of penniless shabby—gentility, repeated failure as a would—be author, humiliation as a rejected time-server. These are, probably, the dominating traits which appears to have a significant influence in grounding his conceit out of him, and forced him to be 'self-sufficient' and to understand that such man as he is. The world will give nothing that he cannot take from it by force (Shaw: 801). It seems that, when Shaw insists on making his hero so like himself, the character has more reality in the stage direction rather than in the play. Another way of using one's own personality is to make of it the measuring—rod for what is not oneself: one can measure *difference* with it as well as *likeness*. In this point, also Shaw differs from a sound historian not in being more subjective only but also in not being, as we can tell, a historian at all. It can be safely hypothesized that his has a task—the task of a literati to air the voices of poetic justice—not to tell anything of historical veracity. It is, therefore, evident that Shaw has taken off all the halo, all the illusion that the romantic writers have credited him with and like Constant, Premier Valet de Chamber, (in his *Recollection of the Private Life of Napoleon*, an English translation of which appeared in 1895 which Shaw appears to have read), he has depicted Napoleon *endeshabille*, as a man, a greatman, still a mere man, not a demigod, and no wonder he has been accused of having given a distorted picture of the great emperor.

From the above discussion, it appears that Shaw's Napoleon possesses almost all the ingredients of the Shavian prescription of a great man realism, originality and will and their non-comitants —fixity of purpose, indifference to personal happiness and dignity, freedom from conscience and moral scruples, disregard for convention and finally control over self. But it appears that the Shavian Napoleon lacks the calmness of a historians' Napoleon.

In making Napoleon susceptible to some of the common weaknesses, Shaw has been quite faithful to history where Napoleon seems to be haunted by jealousy. Shaw's Napoleon, like the Napoleon of history, is a conglomeration of greatness and weaknesses. The Shavian view of greatness is that it co-exists with matter-of-factness, timidity weakness of all sorts—an anti-romantic view of the hero.

If we take even a loose definition of history, describing it as 'an interpretation of evidence' (Collingwood: 56), we can not support the historicity of the play. *The Man of Destiny* is constructed on an episode for which there is no historical warrant. The episode, appears to be, designed only to vindicate the intentionally ascribed the Shavian qualities in Napoleon. The incidents are imaginary but the portraiture, seems to be, real.

The incidents and appearances are dramatically satisfactory. *The Man of Destiny* is a faithful study of a historical personage after placing him in an unhistorical situation. A person who contributed to the making of a glorious history is once again, in the Shavian treatment, contributing to the making of a good literary piece. Shaw, appears to have, only, taken into account, in portraying his Napoleon, the dominant traits and qualities of this historic figure to air the Shavian voices in a subtle way. As we all know that Shaw is not a historian but a creative artist, and his emphasis is on character issuing in action, no matter whether the action has a historical basis or not. He himself labelled the play: 'A Fictional Paragraph of History'. Shaw seems to be victorious in inventing a fictitious story for giving a correct and convincing picture of the inner-self of a general, who soon became the Emperor of Europe.

CAESAR AND CLEOPATRA

Caesar and Cleopatra, Shaw's first major historical venture, presents Cleopatra *vis-a-vis* Caesar and not Antony as in Shakespeare and Dryden. He drew upon Mommsen's *History of Rome* and Plutarch, but Caesar is also to some extent, a self-portrait. As distinguished from the romantic and superstitious Egyptians here he appears to be a hard headed, down to earth, practical man who refuses to be swayed by romantic notions like love, revenge, heroic gesture, etc. Thus, as is apparent, the Shavian Caesar is not a slave to lust as was Shakespeare's, rather a great man with tremendous control over his passion, allowing no woman, not even Cleopatra, to exercise any influence over him when there was a grave task ahead of him. Taking assistance from Mommsen, Shaw has shown the love between Caesar and Cleopatra as a trifling affair, flouting all classical authorities. Shaw takes up Caesar's Egyptian war, the most difficult and dangerous war Caesar had ever undertaken, for the theme of his drama. As Roman consul, Caesar arrives in Egypt to settle a dynastic dispute between young Ptolemy and his sister—wife Cleopatra and to exact the tribute the father of the two rivals owed to Rome. Soon he finds himself entangled in a dangerous conflict with the Egyptian soldiers, the city mob and the Roman army of occupation under the leadership of Achillas.

He is in a foreign country vastly out numbered by a well equipped and cunning enemy, the north west wind prevailing at this season of the year is unfavourable to him; all his communications by sea have been cut off and he has been deprived of all drinking water; in a short time he and his troops are faced with the danger of imminent destruction. But though caught off his guard and though without sufficient troops, Caesar by his customary resourcefulness, brilliant improvisation and personal bravery, makes head against a great city and a powerful army, and wins a victory. Ultimately, he collects 16,000 talents, establishes Cleopatra as queen to rule over Egypt under Roman Supremacy, appoints Rufio as the Roman Governor and returns to Rome. In all standard editions of *Caesar and Cleopatra,* Shaw added a sub-title 'A History'. In Mander and Mitchenson we find a sub-title 'A History in Four Acts' and these authors reproduced a 'Day Bill' advertising the play with the sub-title 'A Chronicle play in Five Acts' (58, 65). In defense, Shaw in the *New Statesman,* described his play *Caesar and Cleopatra* as a Chronicle something in the manner of John Masefield's *Tragedy of Pompey the Great* (Shaw: 112-113). Henderson reproduced the programme, which he calls the most elaborate of any of the Shavian plays, of the copy right performance, and this programme yields the subtitle 'An Historical Drama in Five Acts'. Scattered early editions of the play were subtitled 'A Page of History' (Bentley: 163). However, the French translation of Bernard Shaw by Augustin and Henriette Hamon, which appeared serially in the *Revue de Paris* in February and March, 1924 listed no sub-title. The Spanish translation by Julio Brouta (Madrid, 1909), sub-title the play 'Comedia Historica' and Shaw's authorised German translator, Siegfried Trebitsch, called it 'Eine Historisch Komodie' in a separate version (Berline, 1919), although in the Stucke fur Puritaner (Zurich, 1946), the sub-title, 'Eine Historic in Funf Akten' is again based on the standard edition. On 15 December, 1898 when he had just finished the play Shaw wrote to Golding Bright that the play—'is in five acts, containing eight scenes, and involving considerable variety and splendour of mounting' (77). Martin Meisel aptly says about this play: 'Costume and crowds, scenery and spectacle, were thoroughly in the line of the nineteenth century treatment of history on the stage not only as an elementary part of audience but as the adjuncts of a heroic atmosphere' (364).

It can easily be assumed that Shaw likes to label the play as history—more specifically a 'comic history'. Shaw defended himself in his joust with Desmond MacCarthy in part by maintaining that a schoolboy could pass a collation on the Alexandrian episode by reading his play *Caesar and Cleopatra* (Shaw:112-113). To the end, Shaw maintained that more of truth of history could be learned from the text books—a view seems to be more consistent with the conviction that stage is a platform for propaganda. This extra-text veracity, about the historical events makes the scientific historians find a pseudo-historic force in the Shavian interpretation of history. Shaw, on the contrary appears to have doubted the traditional conventions of scientific historiography. For example, we may refer to gentleman Johnny Burgoyne's answer to Major Swindou's anguished query about Saragota—'What will history say? with the sarcastic rejoinder 'History, Sir, will tell lies as usual (III: 67). In *Geneva* the Judge speaks of 'falsehoods called history (III: 81). *In Everybodys Political What's What ?* Shaw contends that *In Good King Charles's Golden Days* will teach the dynamics of Charles's reign 'better than a decade of grubbing in the British Museum' (181). It is evident from the above discussion that Shaw was merely putting first things first to satisfy the demand of history. In this case no one needed to be told that the history was comedy; everybody needed to be given a reminder that the comedy was history. There, probably, was no problem here any how; Shaw's sub-title may be translated to mean simply that he, like so many others from Aristotle on, held poetry to be superior to history; or that, for Shaw as for the Middle Ages, comedy was a vehicle of moral instruction; or that with Bunyan whom he so much admired, he saw literature as propaganda. So it seems to be justified when Henderson describes the play as 'fantasy', as anticipated by J.G. Huncker: 'It is all truth—telling on a miraculous plane of reality, a reality which modulates and merges into fantasy' (Henderson: 248). In *Caesar and Cleopatra*, it is not unlikely that, one may find more of Masefield than historic Pompey just as the 'Shavian Caesar has more of Shaw' (Trewin: 49). Here, as is apparent, the Shavian hero, however, gives his play a focus that might more fairly remind us of Shakespeare's *Henry-IV* and *Henry-V,* with whom Shaw's Caesar has been compared (Charlton: 19–24).

Further, the play is enriched with a Prologue and an 'Alternative to the Prologue', probably, to highlight the contrasts. The Prologue expounds the relevant chapter of Roman history in terms of Caesar *versus* Pompey, and this in Shaw's view, perhaps, means the creative man versus the rule—bound soldier. Caesar is figured not as the complex patrician but as a classless adventurer who makes up his own rules as he goes along. These two types are of course reconciliable but Shaw, as is apparent, simplifies greatly. Julius Caesar's actual *bon vivant* tendencies, his prodigality, his positive sensual love for Cleopatra, and his general sensuality, his 'covetous desire to be king' as Plutarch puts it, even his zest for soldiering: all these features and more are wilfully eliminated or played down. Nevertheless, the real Caesar's unassuming meatiness remains in the play and his all-important replacement of convention by common sense.

In the Prologue Shaw also proclaims that since the 40's BC there has been no significant improvement in the human race. Shaw believes that men are pretty well as they have been throughout recorded history, but here and there an Alexander or a Caesar or (a Shaw?) rises above his fellows. The 'Alternative to the Prologue' merely though plausibly shows the Superstitious terror and war-like ethos of the Egyptians of Cleopatra's day. Presumably these are not the features we have positively outgrown so much as ancient parallels to our own savage ways.

The five acts of the play itself are integrated in terms of narrative but thoroughly provided with historical details as regards their chief purpose, the portrait of Caesar. It may better be called a history play in Ibsen's or Herman Hettner's sense of a work based on history but primarily of psychological and ethical relevance to the author and his contemporaries. Shaw, seems to have believed that his Caesar was more or less the Caesar of history but the character appears to be a Shavian valuation of himself at his best. That is to say, Caesar behaves as Shaw would have wished to behave in the same circumstances. Naturally, in projecting his ego-ideal Shaw, probably, is setting up a hierarchy of values. Caesar—therefore Shaw—occupies the pinnacle and this is not so much a sign of vanity as a recognition that the great un-Caesarian or un-Shavian mojority are enslaved by their habits of mind and body and caught in cultural snares. For that very reason, probably, there rests a probability whether the Shavian Caesar is substantially more than a critic of society, for his solution to problems are simply unprejudiced and perhaps objectively correct.

Shaw's departure from the recorded history can easily be discerned if a space is provided to analyse the Shavian effort to fictionalise the historical characters, specially the character of the protagonist—Caesar, round whom the action of the play centres. In *Caesar and Cleopatra* Shaw appears to have made an frantic effort to portray a truly great man. The Shavian Caesar is thus a man of outstanding qualities and power; he is a master not only of his mind but also of his environments; he has a purpose of his own and he appears to be, endowed with a tremendous will which enables him to manipulate things and beings for the accomplishment of his purpose. He seems to be immuned from the weaknesses which lower mortals are heir to; he is, says Shaw; naturally great. 'Shakespear's Caesar might have been a successful importer of bananas: Shaw's is a genius whose every speech has the sound of a genius' (Ervine: 364). But the greatness of Caesar here, perhaps is revealed through a number of contrasts. In the first three acts, Caesar is Cleopatra's teacher, teaching her how a queen should behave. In the last two acts she is found to have gained in dignity and wisdom through contact with the greatness of Caesar. But as she develops revengeful and erotic passion, she becomes Caesar's antagonist and stands as a contrast to the protagonist, who has no such passion. The men about Caesar—Rufio, Achillas, Pothinus and others—with their conventional attitudes and irritable temper throw into bold relief Caesar's originality and composure. The contrast between Caesar and Theodotus in their attitudes towards the burning of the library of Alexandria may be seen as a contrast between a maker of history and a historian, between a creator of environment and a creature of environment, between a man of decision and a man who has no decision. About the historical acceptability of his Julius Caesar, Shaw claims, 'Shakespeare's Caesar is the *reductio ad absurdum* of the real Julius Caesar. My Caesar is a simple return to nature and history' (492-493). But the Caesar of Shaw is definitely an artistic creation and seems to be far away from the Caesar of history.

So far as the historicity of the play is concerned; it appears that Shaw remained faithful to the pages of history in describing—Caesar's capture, loss and recapture of the island of Pharos, his swimming for his life, the story of Apollodorus carrying Cleopatra in a carpet to the burning of the fleet, the fire which consumed a great portion of the Alexandrian library, etc.

But the centre of Shaw's interest is not the historical narrative but the character of the protagonist. He is a dramatist who meets the exigencies of the theatre and throws into bold relief the character of the protagonist even by making changes in the historical events. The Shavian Caesar, as is apparent, is too great to find any joy and peace in the terrestrial events. Though as a general, he has to remain constantly busy with wars and conquests, his real self is far from being satisfied with such activities. He, probably, belongs to a different world, as it were, and walks in 'the earth with a sort of stern levity, lightly touching the planet and yet spurning it away like a stone. He walks like a winged man who has chosen fold his wings' (Chesterton; 152). He is, as is evident, intensely conscious of the futility and vulgarity of his occupation as a soldier, and occasionally turns away from reality to leave in contemplation of the constant and immortal part of his life. He is a being apart, and conscious of great superiority to humanity, he feels lonely, as lonely as the Sphinx in the vast Egyptian desert, whom he addresses thus:

> 'Hail, Sphinx: Salutation from Julius Caesar!... Sphinx you and I, strangers to the race of man, are no stranger to one another...' (I: 1–20).

The Sphinx may also he considered to symbolise the genius of Caesar: 'part brute, part woman, and part God—nothing of man in me at all' (I: 37–38). Therefore the dominating spirit in drawing the character appears to be purely artistic in nature. Shaw's Caesar, as a character, seems to be, one of the greatest experiments of the Life Force; as S.C. Sengupta says, 'the evolutionary instinct is never dormant in him' (119). As a disciple of Bergson and Samuel Butler, Shaw was undoubtedly obeying a law of his nature, the same artistic urge, we might add, that draw him to Mommsen and Carlyle; a creative view of evolution was bound to capture Shaw's imagination as had a creative view of history. So it may sound natural that Shaw's Caesar can feel that his great soul is being cramped within the narrow confines of his profession. He is sick of Rome as he is of a warrior's profession. He thus tells Rufio, 'Oh, this military life! This tedious brutal life of action! That is the wrost of us Romans...a swarm of bees turned into men' (IV: 338-341). Apollodorus aptly describes him as not 'merely the conquering soldier but the creative poet artist'. A great creative genius, Caesar loathes war which is a force of destruction. He is a dreamer and he seems to be ready to pay many things for a beautiful dream. Standing before the Sphinx in the vast moonlit desert, he hears a girl's voice and thinks that he is dreaming and he says to himself: 'What a dream! what a magnificent dream! Only let me not wake, and I will conquer ten continents to pay for dreaming it out to the end' (I: 60–63). Here, he seems to behave like a visionary, longing to build a new kingdom, a holy city free from the vulgar pursuits of this world. He cries out, 'Cleopatra: will you come with me and track the flood to its cradle in the heart of the regions of mystery?...Shall I make you a new kingdom, and build you a holy city there in the great unknown?' (IV: 610–618). These may be the utterances of a poet and mystic, of historian—in no sense, living an active life but with one part of his soul always looking upward to the ideal world of his dream. Here Shaw, probably, has given us a few fleeting glimpses of this mystic, poetic Caesar, who is so different not only from his fellows but also from himself as he appears to the world.

Shaw appears to have attributed to Caesar the Shavian prescription of great man such as qualities of absolute disinterestedness in worldly affairs, freedom from worldly ambition and aversion to political and military glory. Shaw in his notes following the play says that it is clear from Caesar's whole history that what has been called his ambition was an instinct for exploration. He had much more of Columbus and Franklin in him than of *Henry-V*. In the Shavian treatment, Caesar becomes a wonderful blend of magnanimity and clemency, which may be considered as an offshoot of reality. History provides ample evidence that Julius Caesar had a burning ambition for political and military eminence and glory. Coming upon a statue of Alexander the great in Spain he reproaches himself for having accomplished so little at an age when the Macedonian had conquered half the Mediterranean world. While in Spain he devoted his leisure hours for reading the history of Alexander; this made him very pensive and at last he burst into tears. As his friends were wondering what might be the reason, he said, 'Do you think I have no sufficient cause for concern when Alexander at my age reigned over so many conquered countries, and I have not one glorious achievement to boast' (Langhorne: 235). Plutarch speaks of Caesar's ever increasing passion for fresh renown: 'Caesar had such talents for great attempts, and so vast an ambition, that the many actions he had performed by no means induced him to sit-down and enjoy the glory he had acquired: they rather whetted his appetite for other conquests...and inspired him with a passion for fresh renown, as if he had exhausted all the pleasures of the old. This passion was nothing but a jealousy of himself (as eager as if it had been with another man) to make the future achievements outshine the past' (*Ibid*: 272). But Mommsen who was Shaw's source, has diluted Caesar's rationalism with occasional mysticism and his worldliness with a tinge of unworldliness. Shaw has taken a hint from him and transformed the ambitious adventurer, Caesar, into an unworldly mystic, an exile into this world which he spurns. The veracity of history has been shaken severely when R.N. Roy says that Shaw has drawn a portrait of himself in Caesar by representing him as an unworldly man, a dreamer dreaming of perfection not to be found in this universe. But in this silly chaotic world, Shaw was a man of business sagacity, sufficient to himself and strong enough to dispense with happiness. The trait of Shaw's character is also seen in Caesar. Caesar, whose deeper self loves to turn away from this world, is found to be adroitly busy with the affairs of the world. These two contradictory elements have been blended together in the character Caesar (Roy: 30-31). Caesar's fatherly appearance to both Ptolemy and Cleopatra may be considered as extra-text reality.

In delineating Caesar's character and his relationship with Cleopatra, Shaw has flouted all classical authority. In doing so Shaw has taken, hints from Mommsen:

> 'He (Caesar) had had his reason of youth, and song, love and wine had taken lively possession of his spirit; but with him they did not penetrate to the inmost core of his nature.... Around him, as around all those whom the full lustre of woman's love has dazzled in youth, fainter glimpse of it continued imperishably to linger; even in later years he had love—adventures and successes with woman.... But, however much even when monarch he enjoyed the society of woman, he only amused himself with them and allowed them no manner of influence over him; even his much censured relation with Cleopatra was only contrived to mask a weak point in his political position (Dickson: 307).

It may be noted here that Mommsen makes Caesar's passion for Cleopatra a policy of expediency while Shaw represents this passion as a dream, not an infatuation, which has nothing to do with expediency.

As regards his power to control the instinct of sex and his love episode with Cleopatra, Shaw's picture of Caesar, which is based on Mommsen, is entirely different from the Caesar of history. The virtue of complete mastery over sexual passion which Shaw has attributed to Caesar is, probably, a myth. Ample evidence is provided by classical authorities that Julius Caesar was a man of hot sexual impulses—a dissolute man, gratifying his sex instinct by extravagant and indiscriminate indulgences. Suetonius has given a long list of Roman matrons—wives of Roman nobles whom he had seduced (Graves: 31). Among the mistress says Suetonius, there were also several queens, the most famous among whom was Cleopatra. Scandals about his indiscriminate illicit relation with women clustered thick about him, and many ribald verses were composed and sung throughout Rome. During his Gallic Triumph, the following song was popular:

> 'Home we bring our bald whore—monger;
> Romans, lock your wives away!
> All the bags of gold you lent him
> Went his Gallic trats to pay' (*Ibid*: 31).

History tells that he was involved in many sexual affairs at the same time, and changed his mistress as his fancy dictated. It was rumoured that Brutus was really Caesar's son. Plutarch says that Caesar believed Brutus to be his son. 'Possibly Brutus himself shared this opinion, and hated the dictator for having seduced his mother and made him, in the gossip of Rome, a bastard instead of the Brutus (Durant: 196). Whatever the truth in the scandal, Servilla, the mother of Brutus was the woman he loved best and she held him longer than any other woman, and it was gossiped that in later years she was induced to surrender her daughter Tertia to Caesar's last. Servilla, a woman of insatiable sexual passion, 'Sapped his strength until he was in danger of physical collapse' (Luduig: 33). The real Caesar, it will be evident, is not at all like the man of destiny whom Shaw has credited with tremendous power to control the instinct of sex.

Though Shaw has not attached any seriousness to the love between Caesar and Cleopatra yet he has hinted a completely new picture of love between them. He has made Cleopatra sixteen though, in fact, she was twenty-one at the time of Caesar's arrival in Egypt. According to Mommsen, she was nineteen when Caesar met her for the first time. Shaw may have deliberately made Cleopatra younger by five years, probably, to suggest that the existence of any serious love between a girl of sixteen and an old man of fifty is absurd. Following Mommsen faithfully, he says, through the mouth of Ra, that—Caesar, seeking Pompey in Egypt, found Cleopatra. This event may also be considered as a deliberate falsification so far as the historic chronology of the period is concerned.

In comparison with Caesar, Cleopatra is intentionally of little interest, when we first meet her hiding on the Sphinx she appeared as a sixteen-year-old bundle of wilfulness, credulity and craft. She, as is apparent, never seriously advances beyond that stage but instead learns from Caesar various tricks of dominance. Little of Plutarch's Cleopatra remains and it seems Shaw really saw the historical woman as a capricious Victorian girl. It was so necessary for him to rob Cleopatra of the variety and power usually attributed to her: that celebrated compound of animal cunning, persistent ruttishness, genuine affection, regal authority, theatrical talent, delightful conversation and savage cruelty—the whole enveloped, at suitable times, in cloth of gold luxury. But Shaw, as is apparent, dismissed as total fable what must have been only the distortions and simplifications of a legend. His Cleopatra is designed to demonstrate his Caesar's easy superiority.

Several of other historic people are brief serviceable character—sketches. Ptolemy Dionysius is no more than a misfit, a normal boy forced into the role of king. Shavian Ptolemy supersedes his chronological age, only when, he comes out with an illuminating comment: 'It is not the lion I fear, but the jackal' to Caesar's apprehension: 'Here you are in lion's mouth'. It may also be safely prognosticated that Theodotus is a minor satire on the figure of learned man at court, quick, pretentious, spiteful; Pothinus appears simply as a sharp, head-strong fellow, for his eunuchism is of no account.

Rufio, probably, is more substantial the Shavian counterpart of Shakespeare's Enobarbus before the letter's doubts set in at Actium. And as Enobarbus verifies the fascination of Cleopatra and the self-betrayal of Antony, so Rufio's bluntsness enhances Caesar as the supremely self-confident captain with whom it is never necessary to be tactful. Lucius Septimus may represent the martial code which Caesar finds offensive. What is interesting about him is, perhaps, his flat, unruffled acceptance of traditional ways: he kills Pompey because 'woe to the vanquished' is the natural law. Losers are automatically killed or enslaved.

Ftatateeta, Cleopatra's nurse appears to be a striking historical realisation because of her ancient, uncomplicated delight in master-slave distinctions and blood-lust cruelty. A victim is purely a regalement, and of course one might be a victim oneself. In the 1890s Ftalateeta must have required a nice enough exercise of the historical imagination and it is doubted that the twentieth century has brought the type back to life, for the murderousness Shaw depicts here, as a feature of the ancient world still seems too unevolved and animal—pure for modern times. Ftatatecta would rather die or suffer unspeakable pains herself than think ahead, take precautions, check her instinctual drives.

Shaw, who could create such a convincing creature, never the less could not resist such anachronisms as Apollodorus and. more blatant still, Britannus. The latter's incongruousness was denied by Shaw yet it appears to be improper to argue that such a stuffy, face-saving, post-1850 gentleman could have been found in the forests of Gaul. Apollodorus, the young patrician peacock, practitioner of art for art's sake, who happens more over to be daring, chivalrous and skilled with the sword, is, perhaps, Shaw's amiable picture of an Alexandrian nobleman. As an artist he is a 'famous patrician amateur' and therefore acceptable to Britannus. But in truth, Apollodorus appears to be simply Elizabethan (May:162–164).

It is evident from our discussion that Shaw has taken sweeping liberties with recorded history and has given a personal interpretation so far the characters in the play are concerned. The immediate source of Shaw's *Caesar and Cleopatra*, as we all know, is Mommsen's *History of Rome*. Mommsen was a German liberal, disillusioned, as. Shaw had been, just after the Marxist failure in England, by the muddles and humiliations of the German revolution of 1848-1849. Writing shortly after the revolution, he felt the needs for great man to bring order out of chaos created by the failure of the German people to realise its political aspirations. He, therefore, idealised Caesar, probably, to impress upon his countrymen that a strong man was needed to save Germany from ruin. Mommsen, in actuality, is a judicious historian but his account of Julius Caesar appears to be panegyric and many of his statements are in contradiction to the classical as well as modern authorities. Shaw has taken some hints from Mommsen, but in his representation of Caesar as a man without worldly ambition and, especially, in his treatment of the relation between Caesar and Cleopatra, which, probably, is the main theme of the play, he has got from Mommsen only slight hints, if hints they might be called, and appears to have idealised Caesar by exaggeration and often, turning facts topsy-turvy. This idealisation seems to be a product of his professed purpose to draw the picture of a Superman from the pages of history just as Mommsen's idealisation is the product of his yearning for a strongman to solve effectively the problems of Germany. In this juncture it may be safely hypothesised that Shaw's Caesar is doubly removed from actual history—once by Mommsen and then by his own calculation.

It is apparent from the current discussion that the Shavian Caesar is not a faithful portrait of a historical character. Shaw in this play has given, perhaps, a portrait of a great man of his conception, a portrait which, judged by the consistency of the portraiture and the piquancy of its relationship to general truth is convincing. Compounded of an indomitable will, an ability to influence other people and a capacity to accomplish his purpose, Caesar appears to be an extraordinary man and he occupies a very prominent place in the portrait gallery of Shaw. He seems to be a fine realist, a sublime artistic creation and it sounds almost immaterial that he is not a replica of the Caesar of history.

SAINT JOAN

Saint Joan is regarded as one of the best plays of the twentieth century and probably the greatest historical drama since Shakespeare. Shaw claims it to be a perfect historical play and it does not merely dramatise an abstract theme like the historical plays of John Drinkwater. In fact, the figure of Joan has been the target of sentimental effusion through ages and a vague response to the charm of a maddeningly heroic girl is the accepted code. Shaw, seems to be, aware of the difficulty of creating a Joan who does not conform to the popular imagination and at the same time he was, perhaps, conscious of the mess into which the previous authors had landed themselves. The playwright is confident that a historical character of the stature of Joan should not be distorted rather he has been willing to bring out the real significance of Joan. Shaw's response to history is analytic and nobody should imagine that Joan really talked in the way Shaw makes her talk. The Shavian interpretation is based on the law of probability and he, perhaps, points out the quintessence of the character by making her the unconscious voice of Protestantism before Martin Luther and thus, finally makes her the symbol of a force in history. This play, says Shaw, sets up a standard which uplifted many young women 'beyond vulgarity and meanness' (West: 245).

The story began while Joan of Arc was little more than a child still living on her father's farm. She began to see visions and to hear voices which were not human, and she became convinced that she was being visited by Saint Catherine and Saint Margaret and Saint Michael. She believed that she is ordered by the Almighty about her future course of action.

'I hear voices, telling me what to do. They come from God' (I: 374-375). When she went to tell the army officers and the priests and the king about the visions and voices, about the mission she was commanded by them to carry out, the officers laughed at her, the priests were horrified, and the weak and lazy young king thought her a nuisance. The priests were quite sure that the Christian Church was the only channel through which God's will could be known. They were so certain of this that they said Joan's voices must come from the devil and were therefore evil. The conflict between Joan of Arc and the Christian Church, thus, was a conflict between Private Judgment and Constituted Authority.

In the first four scenes of *Saint Joan* Shaw dramatises the French National Movement and in the last two scenes he shifts his ground and dramatises what he states in the Preface: 'The conflict of the Regal, Sacerdotal and Prophetic power, in which Joan was crushed' (622).

Shaw asserts that his *Saint Joan* also presents a historical picture, faultless and complete in all details. This claim of historicity has been hotly contested and attempts have been made by critics to 'save history from Shaw' (Robertson: 40), just as Shaw is said to have written the play to save the Maid from Mr. Drinkwater. Desmond MacCarthy, David Daiches, S.C. Sengupta, C.B. Purdom, G.G. Coulton categorised the play as pseudo-historic (1). On the otherhand, Archibald Henderson, St. Joan Ervine, Charles Wayland Lightbody consider the play as amazingly close to historic fact (2). Keeping all the captions in mind it may be safely hypothesised that Shaw, here, is boldly romancing, to his own confusion. He is ostensibly assuming that what he likes to call the literary representation of the Maid, as was the case with Voltaire and Schiller and Southey in poetry and drama. The play, basically, represents all the incidents already known to the common public. But it is apparent that the royalist glorification of the Maid was only politically interrupted at the French Revolution. Literary, history tells us that a dozen of French and English historians before Quicherat had presented her seriously, eulogistically and yet rationally. Quicherat, who for Shaw, said to have, put things on a new footing, is for Anatole France the type and leader of the modern free thinking historians, who as he puts it, indulges in 'a ridiculous exaggeration of Jeanne's intellectual faculties' (Robertson: 22–33).

Shaw, after a thorough search, invents that the rationalist and materialist historian are contemptuously hostile to the Maid. He, perhaps, took up this sentiment as a needed foil to his own neo-romantic attitude. Anatole France, the self-styled rationalist and materialist historian of the present day, sees historical events in the attitude taken up by Shaw. Shaw, on the other hand preferred to call himself a belated pupil of Quicherat—the sentiment-free thinker, and finds satisfactions in recognising the essentially religious character of the Maid's action and influence, inventing or reinventing a doctrinaire figure which has no historical actuality.

The most distressing aspect of the debate, as is apparent, is that Shaw, who holds himself as nothing if not innovating, is merely reviving what had become the patriotic-philosophic view in France before Hume and before the publication of Voltaire's

Pucelle. Supernaturalistic view of history had, perhaps, been expelled from consideration by a group of less combatant thinkers. Therefore, it appears that the exploitation of Jeanne's soul by the priests could not get enough air. But to consider Anatole as the ideal historian, for which he, probably, could not qualify himself, we may find ourselves critically bound to pronounce him right as against Quicherat, though wrong in thinking Quicherat the introducer of the early rationalist view of Jeanne as a born general. That fashion of explanation is applied to history, perhaps, even before the early German rationalists applied it to Biblical miracles. The errors occurred mainly due to the inertness in taking due account of the atmosphere of faith, and thus making a false induction. But Shaw, perhaps, for the first time, fully recognises the personal force of Saint Joan. His final words of dismissal are:

> 'He is not anti-Joan but he is anti-clerical, anti-mystic and fundamentally unable to believe that there was any such person as the real Joan' (628). It may be safely affirmed that under cover of a historic name, here, all the Shavian prescriptions of a great man are ascribed to the character of the heroine. This method may better be called a typical the Shavian way for interpretation of historical events—no argument, no analysis, no weighing of evidence or balancing of detail; but simple pontifical pronouncement, for the edification of his faithful.

It appears that while Anatole's book is at many points open to serious and adverse criticism, Shaw's method is, in one way or other rests at a safe distance from their fangs. It, probably, imperfectly realises the modern standard of history written with the discursive pre-occupations of the popular litterateur, it sacrifices much to the aim of popularity; and it outgoes historical warrant when it treats as a certainty, after putting as a conjecture, the inference that Jeanne in her early teens had been influenced by a priest or priests who calculated that she could be utilised by them. But such deflections from historic science are, perhaps, as nothing to Shaw.

Let us examine, briefly, the historiography of Joan to show how she had been alternately debunked and exalted. A short study in contrast between Voltaire's poem *La Pucelle* (v-1730), and Schiller's *Die Jungfrace Von Orleans* (1801), may help us understand the spirit. Voltaire, as is apparent, ridicules miracle—mongering and saint worship and impishly turns Joan into a bouncing chamber maid whose seduction is the primary aim of English strategy. Ribald seems to be satirical and extravagant. Voltaire deviates from history by marrying Joan off Dunois and ending the poem with their wedding. Schiller, as is apparent, is a corrective to Voltaire's farcical irreverence and his maid does not die at the stake, but at the battlefield, idealised beyond recognition. Nor did Mark Twain's serious fictionalised biography please Shaw. Twain's *Personal Recollections of Joan of Arc* (1896), transforms Joan into a sweety pathetic child Saint and Cauchon into an obese butcher. Tom Taylor's *Joan of Arc* (1871) was, probably, a popular melodrama not far removed from Twain in spirit with a spy in place of Cauchon as the stage villain. Percy Mackaye's *Jeanne d'Arc* (1906), seems to be a pre-Raphaelite reconstruction and Joan is a recognisable cousin of Yeats's wistful Countess Cathleen. Shakespeare's *Henry-VI Part-I* presents Joan as an agent of diabolical power, a harlot-witch who owes her victories to the devil. French liberal historians like Jules Michelet were largely sympathetic to the Middle Ages. In writing *Saint Joan* Shaw, probably, had all these in mind.

So, it may sound natural that Shaw will mix fact with fiction to satisfy his artistic aim effectively. He is free to tell that 'anti-clerical lies' have been told against the Maid, has given in his play a willfuly false account of her final abjuration and of the execution. He presents Joan as abjuring in fear of life imprisonment, whereas she was ready to face that provided she was not left in English hands. He, as is apparent, represents the execution as forced on at the orders of his burlesque English Chaplain immediately at the close of the trial, whereas the death sentence upon Jeanne's resumption of the male attire which was purposely left in her way. It was on that score she was pronounced a relapsed heretic, and condemned to death. On the point on which Shaw specially differs from Anatole France, the military faculty of the heroine, he puts in her mouth propositions as to the vital importance of artillery for which he seems to have not a shadow of authority save the naive expressions of old chroniclers, and of soldiers like D'Alencon, who did not mean what he means and whom he and Hanolaux absurdly misconceives (Hanotaux: 69). Shaw, as is apparent, calmly disregards the evidence that artillery had played a large part, on the French side, in the siege of Orleans, and some part even in the Battle of the Herrings, before Jeanne was heard of. He has just stopped short of telling us that she received revelations on the importance of artillery from St. Michael.

To such liberties, the dramatist may lay claim as a dramatist. But, taking them, he is not at liberty, under cover of his own fiction, to pose as a historian entitled to flout a more responsible investigator who is really seeking objective truth. From the latter function, Shaw is of course constitutionally averse. Truth for him, as we can assume, never means the intellectual residuum left after application of all the critical tests. It is the pre-possession, the sentiment or sentiments with which he set out, or which arise in him on the way, as and when he is moved to flout some contemporary sentiments. Anatole's effort to shift the value of source and evidence is continuous and capable. Shaw does not recognise that in such matters documentary evidence needs shifting at all. He either accepts blindly or rejects blindly, according as his pre-possession dictates or his historic guide leads. In case of incidental incongruities, he only, as is apparent, glances on the legendary outlines and ignores all historical inquiries. He preferred to frame a knowing solution on the lines of his own unassisted intuitions as to how anything or everything happens, and produce for his receptive auditory an explanation which sweeps aside at once the suppositious rationalist historian and the pietist. All this is, perhaps, just one of Shaw's view's, put without his rhetorical embellishments, and with a simple concern for historic exactitude.

In *Saint Joan*, all the character are historical—Joan, Charles, Warwick, Peter Cauchon, Dunois, La Hire, Robert de Boudricourt, Stogumber, Courcelles, Giles de Rais, Promoter D'Estivet, Inquisitor Brother John Lemaiter, the Executioner, etc. The portrayal of Joan's career is, as it appears, replete with historical particulars—her illiteracy, craze for military life, visit to the squire of Baudricourt, recognition of Dauphin, meeting Dunois, coronation of Charles, her capture by the Burgandians, trail and execution. The study of character, appears to have been marked with a keen sense of dramatic skill, although the characters are made to follow the Shavian prescriptions strictly. Though his characters are transcribed from history, Shaw, as is apparent, endowed them with originality and has given them a larger —than—stage life which is essential to versimilitude. The Earl of Warwick appears to be a perfect representative of the feudal aristocracy and English nationality, yet he is far more than the lay figure he would have been were he that alone, he only performs the task which Shaw permits him to do or tell. Fearing that Joan might undermine the feudal system by establishing her neo-nationalism and making the king absolute autocrat, he gets her arrested and hands her over to Cauchon, as is required by the plot; Shaw, probably, has given us a glimpse of his other interests which have nothing to do with which the play is concerned. His pre-occupation with the well-placed columns of 'rich black writing' in beautiful borders and illuminated pictures cunningly inset in a 'bonny book' in the English tent in Sc-IV, perhaps, reveals an aspect of life which is not connected with feudal statecraft.

Shavian Dauphin is, as is perceptible, allowed to function in an independent way irrespective of his historical stamp. The Dauphin, as history tells us, is a weak, stupid, petulant ineffectual courtier. But in course of the play, Shaw has made him an admirable figure by putting into his mouth words which in real life he could never have found for himself, '...I did not pull her out of the fire. But I have done less harm than any of you'.

Every character in *Saint Joan*, as may be hypothesised, contributes to the development of the action and has, at the same time, distinctive idiosyncrasies *vis-a-vis* their historic exactitude—Robert de Boudricourt, who helps Joan to proceed to the Dauphin, has no will of his own and like all will—less people he is self-assertive and loud-mouthed and disguises his defeat by bullying the weakling of a steward. Dunois, who surrenders his command to Joan and follows her to relieve besieged Orleans, lives a rough military life but is, perhaps, endowed with poetic sensibility, which is perceptible in his invocation of the Kingfisher: 'Blue bird, blue bird, since I am friend to thee, change thou the wind for me' (III: 37-38); and his mystic faith in divine miracles makes him surrender the command of the kings army to the Maid. In Shavian treatment, as is apparent, he becomes a ruffian English soldier, who fashions a rude cross for Joan, a bad man is not wholly bad.

It will be better, as we may perceive, to examine *Saint Joan* keeping Shaw's underlying beliefs in mind. For this play, probably, concerns itself with the sort of historical change that makes no essential difference to human life, although the heroine, an agent of the change, lights the way by her character to a 'higher' future. According to Shaw, Joan helped to usher in Protestantism and European nationalism. Neither of these can be said to have been a clear advance on the Middle Ages, but Joan played her part by a sort of innocent and solemn iconoclasm, the very quality that has a chance of edging mankind upwards. By this process, as we can safely affirm, Shaw's Joan becomes knowingly or unknowingly the herald of the Reformation and the nation-state. She becomes also, incidentally, a precursor of Shaw. He is, probably, 'pre-figured' in his own Joan. The historical personage helped to destroy feudalism so that after her and others of roughly her independent kind neither noble nor cleric stood between God and his servant. But that, perhaps, was not Joan's intention, for as Shaw portrays her she just finds herself regularly circumventing the priesthood and has no design to weaken the general authority of the Church.

Thus Shaw, has given us in Joan a genius of profoundly religious temper whose intermittent contact with the 'world', the ways of society, makes her both powerful and vulnerable. The power, as is apparent, lies in the intellectual freedom of her thought, an absolute freedom from social constraint and not that reflex defiance of constraint which is but one mode of slavery. Joan's vulnerable quality is, probably, her ignorance of the ways of man. She cannot tell how mean-minded people feel, how they will long to destroy her (May: 197–203).

The medieval background in *Saint Joan* is fairly comprehensive, so far as the drama is concerned. Shaw, here, suggests the crudity of the age through a number of miracles—the hens laying like mad, Joan's recognition of the Dauphin, the change of the wind, the drowning of Glasdale, her jump from a tower sixty feet high and the fire that did not consume her heart—are all appear to be dramatically satisfactory but do not have a solid historical bearing. The position of the Church and the feudal system are, perhaps, presented through speeches of Cauchon, Inquisitor Lemaiter and the Earl of Warwick. There is even a close resemblance between the speeches of Joan and the records of the two trials. Shaw claims that his vision is normal, for he sees things differently from, and better than other people. Though he has not taken any liberty with his source material, treatment of historical events seem to be unique. One allegation against Shaw was that the Bishop of Beauvais was not as free from personal motives as Shaw represented him to be. But Cauchon's own claim to power and authority was based on the fact that Joan was taken prisoner in his diocese of Beauvais. Nor was he influenced by the English and '...the idea of the trial was not conceived by him but the University of Paris' (Sengupta: 140). Infect he was reproached by the English for his dilatoriness. It was through his intervention Joan was spared the customary torture. He sought the opinions of all the Doctors present in Rouen as well as the opinion of the University of Paris which revealed his anxiety to guard against any miscarriage of justice. Charles Wayland Lightbody has discussed these issues elaborately and opined that it is one of the ironies of history that this man should have gone down alike in popular and in literary tradition as one of the blackest villains of all recorded time, worthy of comparison only with Pontius Pilate, because of his leading part in the trial of the peasant maid from Lorraine, whom one must believe that he, as it appears, regarded her as a heretic and witch, a poisoned sheep which it was a matter of Christian duty to remove before it tainted the whole flock (107). Moreover, Joan's demand at the beginning of the trial for a panel of judges in equal number for both the contending parties would have been as controversial as a trial by Joan's French partisans. Shaw remained loyal to history, perhaps, even in the case of the portrayal of Joan's obstinacy which is evident from the three-page appeal of Pierre Maurice made on 23 May {'...we beg, exhort and advise you to correct your words and submit them to judgement of the Church...' (Barrett: 306)}.

As regards the Rehabilitation the Shavian view, irrespective of historical opinion, was that it was as corrupt as the contrary proceeding applied to Cromwell, that it was really a confirmation of the validity of the coronation of Charles-VII. Shaw's view appears to be indisputable. Charles-VII made attempts to ransom her; the University of Paris expressed the same fear in its letter to Jean de Luxembourg; Charles commissioned Guillaume Boville, a Doctor of Theology, to prepare a Memoir favourable to Joan; Charles commissioned Cardinal d' Estoutville, his near relation, and Inquisitor Brehal, a king's man, to make inquiries. It was alleged that there were legal flaws in the trial: the Records were not authentic; the notaries distorted facts under pressure; though declared an ex-communicated heretic Joan was allowed to receive the Last Sacrament; and finally Joan's abjuration was obtained under duress. But subsequent historical research has convincingly shown that Shaw was essentially correct in the disposition of facts although he put himself in the person of Joan. Some of the judges who had condemned Joan turned to exculpate themselves by incriminating their fellow judges who were dead. Shaw, as it appears, is irrefutable in declaring that he had secured in the only possible way sufficient veracity to justify him in claiming that as far as he could gather from the available documentation, and from his power of divination; the things he represents the three exponent of the drama—namely Cauchon, Lemaiter and Warwick—as saying are the things they actually would have said (Shaw: 632).

Irrespective of popular historical stamp, Shaw's choice of the title *Saint Joan* is, perhaps, not just an ironical suggestion regarding the Church's treatment at her canonization in 1920. The epithet Saint appears to be, in Shavian notion, an emphatic rejection of the conventional notions of sainthood as something based on miracles and expiatory martyrdom. Shaw is, probably, even more skeptical of self-mortification. Schopenhauer has praised Christian above Greek tragedy on the ground that the Christian saint negates his will. Probably, Shaw, it appears, does not share Schopenhauer's belief in human depravity thinks that man is saved by affirming his will. Though the Archbishop denouces Joan's assertion of her will as hubris, the same 'Pride' is for Shaw precisely the source of her Salvation. The sensational aspect of her martyrdom is also dismissed by Shaw as stupidity. In a radio talk*, Shaw begged his audience to forget that she had ever been burned.

Yet, sainthood for Joan, as is apparent, was a serious claim for her eligibility in a Shavian community of great men that included Socrates and Mahomet and even professed atheists like Shelley. The miraculous power which moves Joan, is not, according to Shaw, supernatural; it is superpersonal and rests, probably, outside the realm of logic or reason. In so doing he, perhaps, equates the Life Force or evolutionary appetite with what a theologian would call the will of God. Joan's suffering, thus, is holy, not as expiation, a ritual atonement, but because it is the consequence of her struggle to advance the race. Such a view, probably, offended T.S. Eloit. T.S. Eliot calls Shaw's play: 'one of the most superstitious of the effigies which have been erected to that remarkable woman' (389-390). Indeed T.S. Eliot's *Murder in the Cathedral* may be regarded as an attempt to reaffirm the ecclesiastical ideal of Sainthood in reply to Shaw's challenge. It assumed necessary for Shaw to desentimentalise and de-erotise Joan. Shakespeare presents Joan as a baleful seductive villain in a spy-novel, perhaps, neither Voltaire's adjective 'luscious nobility' nor Twain's 'winsomeness' could satisfy Shaw for using the terms as qualifier before the name of Joan. Shaw altered the notions by emphasizing her craze for soldiering and hemanism and categorising her as a sort of woman that wants to lead a man's life. T.W. Robertson who, perhaps misconceived the ides of Joan's Protestantism as a typical Shavian Jeu d' espint did not understand that the term

---

* *The Listener*. 3 June, 1931, pp. 921-922.

designated the belief of some one who reserved the right to place his private judgments above the authorities of an ecclesiastical court.

A brief examination of the individual episode may help clarify Shaw's intention. The first scene, Joan's encounter with the squire, is, as is apparent, a piece of classical farce, but it makes clear the contrast between a fundamentally will—less person and her power of will. Here, Shaw is, perhaps, satirising popular religious psychology which does not understand Joan's triumph of will over circumstances, and of belief over doubt. Shaw treats this transcendental theme breezily in order to shake the conventionally pious. The courtiers appear rational utilitarian and the Dauphin is a ludicrous creature. Only the Archbishop is an astute statesman who perhaps, realises that the faith that can move mountains is a force to be reckoned with.

When Joan meets Dunois at the Loire, Shaw suggests that the force that impels Joan is the Zeitgeist itself. This power may be objectified as human will in conflict with circumstances. In the Tent Scene (Sc-IV) Joan's anti-feudal nationalism is analysed, perhaps rightly, in the colloquy between Warwick and Cauchon. It is to be mentioned here with concern that in the Preface, Shaw acknowledges the anachronism of the debate, but the function of the intellectual playwright, Shaw tells us, is to make his figures more intelligible to themselves than they would be in real life. In a sense broader than Aristotle's, Shaw insists that drama should be more philosophical than history. This philosophical meaning will be clear if we look at the play in relation to the conventional idea of tragedy. There may remain a question— '... Is Shaw's philosophy of the Life Force compatible with the idea of tragedy at all (Sylvan: 888-889). If the tragic drama is a drama of despair, obviously Shaw's is not. Plato thought tragedy demoralising because it fostered the emotions of grief and fear; Karl Jasper says that the cultivation of a tragic sense can lead to self-exaltation which is actually a form of self-indulgence. Even Hegel places a tragedy of ideological conflict like *Antigone* above in play of personal misfortune like *Oedipus*. Shaw, perhaps, wants to substitute the tragedy of despair by a tragedy of faith. To this end, the play appears to be Hegelian and by implication anti-Aristotelian and anti-Shakespearean. Joan's pride and lack of 'prudence' are, probable defects in the character which merely humanise her; and pride is for Shaw a virtue of the superior individual, the agent of the Life Force. Shaw also reminds us that Shakespear had no heroes, that is men with a positive social or religious philoshophy. Perhaps, Shaw was not interested in writing a Hegelian tragedy, though *Saint Joan* is seemingly Hegelian in its treatment of hiostorical processes dramatising evolving forces of nationalism and individualism. Both ruled out personal elements and crime; both stressed, as is apparent, the fatal disagreement between two moral imperatives. Therefore, from dramatic point of view, Joan's trial should not be seen as popular melodrama, but as the confrontation between two antagonistic historical forces objectified and depersonalised. Shaw, perhaps, enters into the mentality of the Inquisition sympathetically, but he does not seek to exonerate it. It is merely to make his point that the most nefarious institutions always seem perfectly justified in their won eyes. Shaw declares that a historian who would defend Joan's burning would defend anything. He forces us to consider the trial from the perspective of fifteenth century, not because he thinks the Inquisition right, but because the fifteenth century regarded it as perfectly respectable. His intention is to warn us that it is just the saintly old men who make the most dangerous apologies for judicial crimes. The ironical rhetoric of Shaw's inquisitor condemning heresy is identical with that of the defenders of our present day laws on sexual offences, obscenity or drug-taking. Shaw calls him a most nefarious scoundrel, because his conviction is that through censorship, expiatory punishments and cruel measures can the human race be civilised.

The defeats of Prometheus are the staple of tragedy, Shaw wrote in a review in the nineties (18). Joan's life was for him a historical tragedy in the Promethean mould in which all the forces that bring about the Catastrophe are on the grandest scale; and the individual soul on which they press is of the most indomitable force and temper (Henderson: 42). The defeats of Prometheus, looked at from this perspective of history, have a way of loosing their tragic quality. The moment of horror disappears as we observe mankind worshipping what is first feared and hated. The angels may weep at the murder but the Gods laugh at the same. In the Epilogue we hear the laughter of the Gods. The actors of her drama all praise her, but they also flinch at the idea of her return to life. The world will continue to kill its saints and heroes until it has grown to their stature and produce a society of saints and heroes. *Saint Joan*, therefore, may be regarded as the final master piece of a great dramatist—not of a historian—proper—who is willing to think and hope.

NOTES

1. MacCarthy, D. *Shaw*. London: Macgibbon and Kee, 1951.

   Daiches, D. *A Critical History of English Literature*. Vol. II, London: Secker & Warburg, 1960.

   Sengupta, S.C. *The Art of Bernard Shaw*. London: Oxford University Press, 1936.

   Purdom, C.B. *A Guide to the Plays of Bernard Shaw*. London: Methuen, 1964.

   Coulton, G.G. *Inquisition and Liberty*. London: William Heinemann, 1938.

2. Henderson, A. *George Bernard Shaw*. NewYork: Appleton—Century Crofts, 1956.

   Ervine, St. John. *Bernard Shaw*. London: Constable & Co., 1956.

   Lightbody, C.W. *The Judgement of Joan*. Longman, London, 1929.

4 In Good King Charles's Golden Days

In Good King Charles's Golden Days is a scintillating comedy and the episodes tell sufficiently about Shaw's amazing vitality, his mental alertness, his versatility, his wit, his irrepressible comic sense, his grasp of character and his delicate sense of style, keeping the traditional search for historical truthfulness far away. Shaw opines that, this play is not a dramatised chronicle, as was Shakespeare's 'Histories' and familiarity with the events, as expressed in the play, may not assist a student safely through examination. About the origin and perspective of the play the playwrit himself added a note in the Preface to avoid misunderstanding: '...In providing a historical play for the Malvern Festival of 1931, I departed from the established practice sufficiently to require a word of explanation' (887). His 'explanation' is, as is apparent, basically a Shavian challenge to current thought and doctrine and contradicts the existing concepts. Unlike other Shavian Histories, Shaw, here, comes out with a different pen. He has, perhaps, laid aside his dogmatism, as is the case with his pugnacity. Shaw, in this play, appears to be a different person with no particular philosophy to preach. He bids good bye to all positive doctrines, pronouncing no verdict, working out no philosophical system but pleasantly chatting on diversified subjects—religion, art, science, king craft; and a number of *obiter dicta* about life, about the still small voice of conscience, of beauty and design, about the function of wives and mistresses—add grace and charm to the discussion.

In Good King Charles's Golden Days is perceptively, pre-occupied with the ideas each are not at parity with the general philosophy. The play appears to be ignorant about plot and character, generally curious about expressing opinions on various problems from a Shavian point of view. It is, after all, the Shavian fancy that dictates the dramatic development.

Shaw has, as is apparent, utilised the popular stage tricks to write a romantic history. He categorised his play as a '...historical romance, mostly fiction with historical names attached to the stock characters of the stage' (887). So, naturally, there remains ample scope to narrate falsified histories or political economy, which Shaw appears to have exploited sufficiently. This deliberate falsification is, perhaps, introduced with a purpose and not just to please his audience. From Macaulay to Hilaire Belloc, the story of Charles-II and his mistresses had been told in different voices. So this time, probably, people wanted to listen a different type of interpretation. And it was now Shaw's turn to air an intellectual tension to satisfy his admirers. So, perhaps, he turned from the sordidness of Charles's reign and his Solomonic polygamy, '...to what might have happened to him but did not, the situation becomes interesting and fresh' (Shaw: 887). For instance, Charles might have met that human prodigy Isaac Newton and Newton might have met that prodigy of another sort, George Fox, the founder of the morality mighty society of friends, vulgarly called the Quakers. The main interest of the play lies, as it assumes, in the clash of Charles, George and Newton. There is also a latent clash of ideas between all the three and Nelly, Castlemaine and Louise de Kerouallle. The wives and mistresses of Charles-II are included in the plot, perhaps, to relieve the intellectual tension.

The play *In Good King Charles's Golden Days* is a two-act play. In the First Act Shaw assembles in Isaac Newton's house at Cambridge in the year 1680—Charles-II, George Fox, Newton and Kneller; also Charles's mistresses Nell Gwynn, Barbara Villiers, Louise de Kerouallle, Newton's house keeper Mrs. Basham and his maid servant Sally, and Charles's brother James. The four protagonists—Charles-II, George Fox, Newton and Kneller—are leaders in their own spheres of kingship, religion, science and art. They express their views on their respective subjects through a conversation that seems never to come to an end. The Second Act shows a shift in place without disturbing the unity of time and takes us to the boudoir of Queen Catherine of Braganza in New market. The hearty conversation between Charles-II and his queen Catherine is, perhaps, intended to reveal the deeper basis of the relation between the two. The conversation also hints at the comic possibility of the play. About the comic aspects of the play rightly did, as it appears, *The Times* comment on 12 August, 1939 that, '...most of our best authors of comedy today sit at Mr. Shaw's feet...what is the explanation? It is surely that Mr. Shaw is a model dramatist in spite of his pre-occupation with so called ideas, not because of them, and that the secret of his dramatists' impulse is in his irrepressible comic sense'. Shaw, therefore, was chatting on the events, perhaps, to air his opinions over the issues and not to retell a known history twice.

Shaw's account shows a marked deviation from recorded history when he makes all the four protagonists meet together, nor do the happenings in the play have their signatures in the pages of history. Though developing a fictitious story with historical names, Shaw, as is clear, nursing the faith that anyone reading this play or witnessing a performance of it will not only be pleasantly amused, but will come out with a knowledge of the dynamics of Charles's reign; that is, of the political and personal forces at work in it, that ten years of digging up mere facts in the British Museum or the Record Office could not give. So in this fantasia Shaw was, probably, playing with few historical names. Only some events that took place in reality are introduced which is clearly perceptible in the action of the characters *vis-à-vis* their appearances. The introduction of actual happenings in the historical characters may also be accounted for misleading the audience. This is done to absorb, perhaps, a Shavian history with the tales of popular heroes and heroines, respect for whom was automatically guaranteed. This may be explained as an effort to give an extra-text truthfulness of his created characters.

Shaw seems to be historically accurate in describing Charles' special care for his spaniels. That the King was fifty in 1680 is also a fact. His physical appearance, his interest for science, his extra-sensuality and constant pecuniary difficulties are all facts.

We have a solid support to prove the historicity of the above mentioned facts from Richard Lodge:

> '...Not only did Charles never recovered from the financial troubles of his exile and the first year of his reign, he was never able to defray his expenses from his normal revenue. Chronic impecuniosity, always verging upon bankruptcy, and on one occasion actually crossing the borderline, gives the clue to many of the problems of the reign' (11-12).

Encyclopaedia Britannica also supports his interest for applied Science and opening up of a personal laboratory and giving the Royal Society its Charter. These are the facts testified by the famous historians like Macaulay (410), John Richard Green (631), Richard Lodge (11-12), Trevelyan (291), etc.

It is apparent that in delineating dramatic characters Shaw has mixed fact with fiction. His portrait of Charles's carnality in excess is, perhaps, historically true, but to show this sexual infidelity, Shaw introduces many fictitious stories. As is in the story, three of Charles's life-partners—Nell Gwynn, Barbara Villiers and Louise de Kerouálle—appear separately in the library of Sir Isaac Newton at Cambridge. Nelly's complain is that she has been kept waiting in the street too long, but is never ruffled—appears to have no historical warrant. There is no such evidence of the fictitious story such of Barbara Villier's bursting into the room 'in a tearing rage' storming and ranting and accusing Charles of being unfaithful to her a thousand times and the suggestion that he should kill her and 'be happy with that low stage player'. Shaw's ways of seizing the characteristic traits of the three female partners of Charles-II is, perhaps, also unique. His Barbara Villier, as is apparent, is not only famous for her tantrums but, as Charles-II tells Catherine, is a woman who thought of nothing but her body and its satisfaction, which meant men and money. For both, Barbara is insatiable—'Grab, grab, grab' (II: 60). Shaw's Nell Gwynn is portrayed, perhaps, more as an actress than a queen, who has 'the gutter in [her] blood'; she is, as is apparent, far away from courtly demeanors; compliant and adorable and centre of Charles's comfort and peace because 'nothing can make a courtier of her'.

Out and out, she is an authentic historical portrait but her frivolity and excess of intellect as had been mentioned by Shaw could not pass the caustic test of historicity. Louise de Keroualle is presented here as a typical French woman having all the temperamental uniqueness of her race and sex. The episode of her coming to Isaac Newton—the alchemist, to have a love charm which would make Charles love her only and not everybody, is perhaps, only dramatically satisfactory. That Shaw was faithful to history in portraying her sexual hotness is evident from the comment of Richard Lodge:

> '...The very contrast may have helped to attract him [Charles] to the childish, simple and baby face of Louise de Keroualle, a young Breton lady...was an account of her foreign origin by far the most unpopular of the King's mistresses. Charles was no more constant to her than he had been to Lady Castlemaine and from time to time her ascendancy was seriously threatened. But her influence was never completely overthrown, and she continued to be the most influential woman at the English court until Charles's death' (106).

Shaw presents Charles-II as using Louise de Keroualle as an agent for extracting money from the king of France giving 'little enough in return'. Here, Shaw appears to have taken outrageous liberty with history. The truth, perhaps, is that Louise de Keroualle was sent by Louis-XIV to act as his spy on Charles-II. She became the most influencial woman in the English court and succeeded in winning Charles-II to French interests. Louis-XIV recognised his obligations by conferring upon her the valuable fief of Aubigny. She, perhaps, represents the continuance of the policy of the Treaty of Dover and the enslavement of England to France. The Shavian departure from the recorded history appears to be deliberate, his purpose being to emphasize Charles's policy of expediency which finds French money as good as English money if little enough is to be given in return for it.

The purpose of telling the story of the three mistresses may be that of reminding the audience about his pre-occupation with the Theory of Life Force as it had been the case with *Man and Superman*. Here also the women are exponents of life-force. Loiuse de Keroualle, though apparently, denies her pursuing of Charles by telling: 'I came to consult Mr. Newton, the alchemist', but her actual purpose, as had been secretly expressed to Newton, was to captivate the king by her physical allurements. The mutual attraction is expressed, only, in the last when she tells that she was sent to England to captivate Charles-II but in this process she had also been entrapped by Charles's 'Seventy niches and [his] good looks'. It may also be assumed here that the encounter of Isaac Newton with the three mistresses of Charles-II is meant to illustrate Shaw's thesis that there lies a bitter conflict in real life between genius and sexual attraction. When Nell Gwynn expressed her willingness to come to him again Newton says: 'No no no no no, Madame, I can not entertain ladies. They do not fit into my way of life' (I: 578-581). The words makes an echo of the Shavian comment in the Epistle Dedicatory of *Man and Superman* to Arthur Bingham Walkely: 'When it comes to sex relations, the man of genius does not share the common man's danger of capture'. This struggle between the genius and the strongest physical passion is beyond the periphery of history.

Shaw, here, presents a Charles who has achieved his fifty. He, in Shavian presentation, is, therefore, a worldly man who has already known much about love and woman and in his consideration: '...the woman themselves are worse penance than any priest dare inflict in you' (I: 621). At a grey-age he could learn that '...bodies are all alike: all cats are grey in dark. It is the soul and the brain that are different' (II: 67–69). Up to this extent Shavian history appears to be at par with the popular history. Majority of the historians have mentioned Charles's profligacy and his neglect and ill treatment of his wife. To support our statement we may cite the account of Trevelyan in this matter:

> '...Catherine of Braganza, an unfortunate woman from a Portuguese cloister, was brought over, married and held up to ridicule by her husband, who compelled her, in spite of tears and fainting fits to employ the Castlemaine as her own lady of the bedchamber' (292).

Richard Lodge also speaks of the brutality with which Charles-II lacerated the heart of the queen to admit Lady Castlemaine as his bed partner. She was subdued and Chartles II stopped ill treating her.

But Shaw, denying all historical warrant, turns the facts of neglect and ill treatment into an episode of happy-compromise. He has represented her resignation to fate as Charles's compassion for much injured wife as genuine love and devotion. Charles's attitude: 'there is nobody like a wife', assists Shaw to project Charles's marital relationship, as is opposite to history, as a model of tenderness, appreciation and reverence. This made, as is projected, partnership as 'made for each other' Charles-II paves the way for great compromise by his confession and repentance for treating her inhumanly when he was a young man and tells her: 'We must forget our foolish youth: we are grown up now' (II: 370). He appears to be ready to do anything to compensate for his unfaithfulness. He, therefore, asks, 'Beloved: can anything I can ever do make up to you for my unfaithfulness?' (II: 159-160). But his wife does not mind, as is in the plot, his romantic tomfooleries, for she knows that he can never be unfaithful to her: ' People think of nothing but that, as if that were the whole life. What care I about your women? Your concubines?... They have set me free to be something more to you than they are or can ever be' (II: 162–166). This appears to be a philosopher's task and is very hard for any worldly lover. In the Preface Shaw argues, like a defending attorney with persuasiveness that he has given a correct picture and rendered the Merry Monarch an act of historical justice. It is evident from our discussion that this picture has no relation to reality, and his assertion that Charles-II was the best of the husbands who 'took his marriage very seriously and his sex adventures as calls of nature on an entirely different footing' is pure Shavianism according to which sex is a mere instrument of creation which does not discriminate between marital relation and extra-marital sex adventures.

Charles-II, like Bluntschli and other heroes of early Shavian drama, has a simple boast: 'I keep my head on my shoulders. It take a man of brains to do that' (II: 390–393). The unstated significance of his being fifty years old in the play is suggested by his father's date: 1600-1649. The action of the long first act shows his wit working humanely as well as shrewdly. By creative 'unsettling the minds of George Fox, Godfrey Kneller and Isaac Newton, the king manages to reconcile these gifted fanatics with a skill that makes the first act as much a depiction of the triumph of its hero as the first six scenes of *Saint Joan* were a portrayal of the triumph of its heroine. But the failure of Joan and Charles-II arises, perhaps, not from any defect for which they could be held accountable as individuals, but from an isolation of faculties which Shaw claimed as inherent in man's nature. Since each of them is limited to supplying only one component of a hypothetical higher being capable of uniting their qualities, both characters, as is apparent, finally become specific historical manifestations of Lilith's general metaphysical dilemma.

This play was probably designed to express the Shavian views on some specific issues. Shaw had bitter experience at Schools and the institution called school was in his opinion, the damnable boy prison. The teachers were, in the Shavian opinion, no better than the executioner and obviously the enemy of mankind. Charles-II never paid any serious attention, as was not allowed by Shaw, to the question of education, nor did he ever pass any judgment on the contemporary system of education. Shaw's Charles, as is apparent, is opposed to the kind of education prevailing in schools. He holds that schools are worse than useless and one has to unlearn what one learns there. George Fox, therefore, says: 'I am not schooled and learned as you two princes are! (I: 2042-2043). To this, Charles's reaction is: 'Thank you stars for that, Pastor: you have nothing to unlearn' (I: 2045). Again Charles-II tells Catherine that 'learning Latin is no use: Jack Churchill, who was an ignoramus, is worth fifty Schoolers' (I: 2048). Here, if any where, we hear the voice of Shaw himself inveighing against the prevailing system of education. So it is evident that throughout the play historical Charles is silent and the Shavian Charles is vocal.

In writing this play, Shaw was pre-occupied with one of the greatest political problems of how to choose rulers and prevent them from abusing their authority. Shaw is, perhaps, Platonic in his pre-occupation and he had to advocate the need of education for this purpose. In this play Charles-II tells Catherine, 'No beloved: the problem of how to choose a ruler is still unanswered; and it is the riddle of Civilization' (II: 292-294). Charles-II does not attempt to solve the problem but shrewdly hints at the direction in which an answer can be found when he says: 'I tell you again there are in England, or in any other country, the making of half a dozen kings and councils; but they are mostly in prison. If we only knew how to pick them out and label them, then the people would have their choice out of the half dozen. It may end that way, but not before they are chosen' (II: 296-297). We can assume that Charles–II, being the constitutional monarch might not have aired his views in this way. Therefore, undoubtedly it was an effort of the dramatist to express his own views about his choice of ruler.

By utmost effort, Shaw was able to produce his Charles and through whom he could propagandise his own opinions starting from the superiority of the Scots to the English. His Charles-II tells Catherine that brains 'are no use here: the English will not be ruled; and there is nothing they hate like brains. For brains and religion you must go to Scotland, ... Again he tells her, 'No: give me English birds and English trees, English dogs and Irish horses, English rivers and English ships; but English men! No, No, No.' (II: 472). This appears to be a typical Shavian paraphrase about the English people. It is apparent that in expressing his opinions he had taken refuse in the historical characters, though the characters have to do very little with their historical exactitude. So, even after that, if we have to tell them historic then this history may constitute a new genre, we will like to call them 'Shavian history'.

Sir Isaac Newton, in this play, is a wonderful Shavian creation. In the Preface Shaw tells: 'Not since, Shakespeare made Hector of Troy quote Aristotle has the stage perpetrated a more staggering anachronism' (888). Shaw has taken, as is apparent, outrageous liberty with the facts of Newton's life. It may be safely hypothesised that Shaw makes Newton react in a Shavian make belief: 'I have made Newton aware of something wrong with the perihelion of Mercury.... But I find the perihelion of Mercury so irresistible as laugh catcher...' (888). Shaw appears to be prepared to defend it as a possibility and his ignorance in these matters is also stupendous. He refuses, as is clear, to believe that Newton's system did not enable him to locate Mercury theoretically at its nearest point to the Sun, and then to find out with his telescope that it was apparently somewhere else. The action of the play opens at a beautiful house in the town of Cambridge and the owner of the house happened to be Sir Newton. Once again, history proved itself helpless to search out any such house of Newton at Cambridge. Shaw represents Newton as 'the greatest man alive' in the year 1680, but the fact in that in 1680 he was, almost unknown outside a small circle of friends who had atleast something to do with science. In the words of Macaulay, '...even in the year 1685, his fame, though splendid was only dawning' (410). The principal cause of his world-wide fame—*Principia*, was published in year 1687. Shaw's Newton tells that he has discovered, 'a force in nature which I call gravitation' (I: 2256). In actuality, the idea of universal gravitation remained untold till the publication of the *Principia* in 1687. In this play, Newton refers to his Chronological History of the world to the writing of which he has devoted a substantial period of his life. But Brewster makes it a point that, this chronological history was completed at the time of Newton's death and it was published in 1728' (338). The staggering anachronisms are aslo found in—Newton's awareness of something 'amiss with the perihelion of Mercury,' his horror at Einsteinian curvature, Godfrey Kneller's idea that 'the line of beauty is a curve', which was basically Hogarth's idea expressed about half a century after 1680. The anachronisms spread throughout the plot, makes Lord Keynes justifiably tell: 'G.B.S. allows the characters of his play to be acquainted with works of Newton which were not published until decades later' (107). The comment aptly tells about the Shavian genius but also successfully denies one important point—which is the focus of our discussion, i.e., historical accuracy.

About the origin of Newton episode, Shaw's main intention, probably, was to draw a pen-picture of an 'eternal clash between the artist and the Physicist'. He, therefore, has invented, as is apparent, a collision between Newton and a person by whom he may have played a Hogarth. So, the spirit in designing the episode itself denies the proper spirit of a historian. Shaw, as is apparent, make an apology for this episode by telling: 'For the flash of prevision in which Newton foresees Einstein's curvilinear universe I make no apology. Newton's first law of motion is a pure dogma... Newton in my play is a stage astronomer...an astronomer not for an age but for all time...,' (888).

Let us now examine, Shaw's statement: 'Newton's first law of motion is a pure dogma', from the stand point of Aestro-Physics. According to the Shavian statement, the law do not have a solid scientific base and it appears to be a mere hypothesis. But in reality this law is a universally acknowledged one and a polestar in the vast sky of science. Newton's first law of motion is a reformation of Galileo's law of inertia and states and was first published in 1686, in *his Principia Mathematica Philosophiac Naturatis*. The first law of motion tells every object continues in its state of rest or of uniform motion in a straight line unless compelled by some external force to act otherwise.

The state of rest and that of uniform motion are both examples of zero acceleration. They are, as a matter of fact, the only examples of zero acceleration. The first law tells us, therefore, that in order to change such a state of motion we need a force. If a body is at rest, we will have to apply a force on it to make it move. If a body is moving with constant speed in a straight line and if we want to change its speed, we will have to apply a force on it to make it move. If a body is moving with constant speed in a straight line and if we want to change its speed we will have to apply a force in the direction of motion. If we want to change the direction of motion, we still need a force acting normal to this direction. In case of a circular motion with constant speed, even though the speed does not change, the direction of motion continuously changes. The acceleration in this case is directed towards the centre.

Newton's first law of motion is also a statement about reference frames. For, in general, the acceleration of a body depends on the reference frame relative to which it is measured. The first law tells that, if there are no nearby objects (it is meant that there are no forces because every force must be associated with an object in the environment), then it is possible to find a family of reference frames in which a particle has no acceleration. This frames are called inertia frames and such frames are either fixed with respect to the distant stars or moving at uniform velocity with respect to them (Resnick & Halliday: 81–83). Therefore, history of Particle Dynamics, as well as Aestrophysics, acknowledged the law as a proven theory and not a 'dogma' as had been called by Shaw.

Again, Newton's encounter, in this play, with Kneller, George Fox and James reveals that he is a proud, vain and ill-tempered person. The recorded history acknowledges Newton's consciousness about his own greatness and his place as a 'philosopher' (Brewster: 338), but it does not acknowledge the pride in his knowledge, vanity, arrogance and irritability which appear to be a Shavian addition to this character. From the biography of Sir Isaac Newton, it is evident that the social character of Newton was such as might have been expected from his intellectual attainments. He was modest, candid and affable, and without any of the eccentricities of genius, suiting himself to every company, and speaking of himself and others in such a manner that he was never even suspected of vanity (Brewster: 337). Dr. Pemberton's daily experience with Newton makes him tell that neither Newton's extreme great age, nor his universal reputation had rendered him stiff in opinion, or in any degree elated. He was extremely modest, and his modesty arouse out of a consciousness of what a small portion of nature had been able to examine and how much remained to be explored. Shaw, therefore, makes his Newton tell: 'I spend my life contemplating the ocean of my ignorance. I once boasted of having picked up a pebble on the endless beach of that ocean. I should have said a grain of sand' (I: 379–381). Chronological history tells that Newton uttered this statement a short time before 1727. Shaw, appears to have, altered the words of this memorable sentiment which had been recorded thus: 'I do not know what I may appear to the world; but to myself I seem to have been only like a boy playing on the sea shore, and diverting myself in now and then finding a smoother pebble or a prettier shell than ordinary whilst the great ocean of truth lay all undiscovered before me' (Brewster: 338).

Thus, *In Good King Charles's Golden Days* Shaw, as may be safely affirmed, proves himself to be a master of anachronism, contradiction and distortion so far as the historical events are concerned. Shaw sacrifices external truthfulness, perhaps, for the sake of revealing the dominant traits of age he lived in. The essence of the story, therefore, is pivoted round to what might have happened but did not. For example, Charles-II might have met Newton, and Newton might have met George Fox. The wives and mistresses are added to the main story, probably, to ease intellectual tension. After all, this play tells about 'a true history that never happened'—a corollary from the Shavian vision of history.

Conclusion

By the time, Shaw could establish himself as a successful dramatic critic, the theatre in England, as was in rest of Europe, had taken a new lease of life. It was a time of prosperity, of the rise of a new middle class and of a new commoners with sufficient time and money to go to theatres and operas. Matinee shows, perhaps, were still a novelty. They were, probably, put on for people who wanted to come up from the suburbs and see the kind of a show. Improved transport made it possible for the continental audience to visit London—theatres quickly and easily. Theatre-going had become respectable as it had been in the Elizabethan period. Such being the vogue of theatrical practice a non-conformist parson of debatable identity did put on an amateur Christmas pantomime in his mission hall without raising the storm of protest that would certainly have followed a few years earlier. The Clergy took upon themselves the chance to preach the possible effective influence of the stage, and praised noble-minded actor-managers who tried to elevate its tone. Shaw, on the other hand, thought that the theatre ought to be 'a factory of thought, a prompter of conscience and elucidator of social conscience, an armory against despair and dullness, a temple of the 'Ascent of Man'. The medieval church used to be the nation's soul. It had, as is apparent, used drama itself to put across its message. This was what Shaw wanted the theatre to be. He believed, as is evident, that a National Theatre was as necessary as a National Church.

On a closer analysis, Shaw found the world riddled with conventions and institutions which had already lost their relevance in a smart society and he carried on a tireless task for a more improved and saner world. He, perhaps, tried to destroy old ideas and useless institutions so that a new world might be created on the basis of rational history. After an acute analysis of contemporary civilization Shaw was, rather, convinced that man as a species had made little progress and that he was doomed if he persisted in his present inadequacy. Man must ever evolve into a higher and higher being if he is not to be scrapped. Greatman, on the other hand, does not follow the beaten track. His outlook on life and the world, his thoughts, feelings and actions are different from those of the general flock. Greatmen prove that it is possible for man to rise to a higher position in the scale of evolution than that which average humanity has attained. They, in Shaw's opinion, symbolise a state of elevated stature what man one day may attain. In the Preface to *Geneva* Shaw says, 'the apparent freaks of nature called Great Men mark not human attainment but human possibility and hope. Further, they prove that though we, the mass are only child Yahoos it is possible for creatures built exactly like us, bred from our unions and developed from our seeds, to reach the heights of these towering heads.' It is evident from the discussion that great men gave him something to look forward to, something to hope for. To get such a greatman in actual life Shaw has, as is apparent, rooted his faith in the legendary figures from the pages of history, ascribing, if necessary, some superman—like qualities to the historical heroes. His historical characters, as may be safely affirmed, are interpreted in the light of his own modern understanding and pre-occupations. The audience witnessing a Shavian history is expected to feel personally involved, or to identify themselves with the characters or their problems. Perhaps for this reason when Shaw wrote his first historical play, Napoleon is presented as thinking and talking in the same way as the audience did. Shaw's Caesar, as is apparent, is human enough for any man in the audience to identify with him. In *Saint Joan*, Shaw, perhaps, has conveyed that Joan is a country girl who talked in the idiom of Lancashire mill-girl. Again, *In Good King Charles's Golden Days* all the important characters are allowed, as is apparent, to behave in a manner average people behave. This type of naturalistic historical plays where the characters think and act and talk in modern idioms was invented and first put into the English stage by Shaw.

In delineating historical characters Shaw, as is universally acknowledged, was not interested in the dark side of human nature. What impressed him much was not the madness of mankind, but its stupidity. Shaw's plays exhibit, probably for the reason cited above, a view of life which is so far from reality that one thinks of them as fables. It is evident that in presenting them as authentic 'natural history', Shaw was thinking of the underlying motives rather than the realism of the demonstration. These motives, perhaps, are rooted in a purely philosophic conception, for Shaw made no effort to sound the depths of the soul below the rational threshold. His 'histories', therefore, go only a little way beyond common sense; but on this level, they have their truth; and in comparison with what ordinarily passes for truth in the theatre, it is at first sight dazzling. In the Shavian postulation, great drama is, as is apparent, directed first of all to the intellect and results in an intellectual experience to which all other pleasures of the theatre are ancillary. This search for intellectualism in art, perhaps, motivated him to a considerable degree to become a unique historian.

In writing historical plays, Shaw was, as is evident, not concerned with historical perspective, with the past as distant and radically different from the present. The sense of genuine cultural remoteness affecting ways of thought in the past is minimised by the dramatist. Shaw was, perhaps, confident that 'time—past' is an important determinant in changing the present. The conflict in which a Joan, or a Galileo, or a Christ was crushed has been going on since pre-historic time. Shaw had derived from Marx a sense of the value of history, of the coherent interpretation of the past as a political determinant, and is concerned with the relation between man's view of the universe and his behaviour in the present. He, perhaps, regards the course of history as flexible and subject to salutary modification by the well meaning will. He rejects, probably, the deterministic approach to history which implies a process of evolution towards a pre-determined goal in which greatman plays a very limited part. Shaw's method is, thus, a Shavian interpretation of evidence. He, therefore, may not place the historical figure in the centre of historical forces, and often place him in an unhistoric situation like the encounter between the Man of Destiny and the Strange Lady.

It is said that Shaw took many liberties with History. His faith in the contemporary age of reason helped him approach historical characters with pre-conceived notion, biases and preferences. But these distortions from factual details by Shaw was not fully appreciated by the reputed critics. David Daiches opines that Shaw might not have understood the characters in their true spirit, for he lacked historical imagination; and these characters became in his hands modern Shavian heroes rather than convincing historical characters. Priestly, rather, terrorised people by declaring Shaw 'an intellectual terrorist who is out to propagate intellectual shocks'. As a matter of fact, Shakespeare also, in airing the Tudor views, departed from the full facts in his English and Roman plays, yet gave an overall view of events and people which we accept because it is consistent with itself and vital, and is what we would expect an Elizabethan writer to make of the period concerned. But Shaw, as is apparent, has great faith, perhaps only, in his own theories. He says, 'As a dramatist, I have no clue to any historical or other personage save that part which is also myself' (Pearson: 58). Naturally enough, he has to face the opposition of scientific historians whose yardstick is truth to historical fact and historical probability.

In the last century, Shaw was the unique artist who grapples with the historical facts as they reflect upon the mind of a sensitive literary artist and hence his treatment of history turns out to be a piece of good literature. As has been a fact with Shaviana, Shaw pays lip-service to conventional realism of popular history, rather magic realism happens to be his favourite mode. Finally the study of the History Plays of Shaw has been an enriching experience with the present author who ends up with the find that more and more emerging areas and scopes on Shaw's notion of historical truth demand further investigation on topics such as form of Shavian histories, their musical pattern of language, Shaw's moral vision, and last not the least on the play—preface inter-relationship.

Bibliography

PRIMARY SOURCES

Advice to a Young Critic. Letters, 1894-1928. London: Peter Owen, 1963.

Bernard Shaw, *W.B. Yeats—Letters to Florence Farr.* Edited by Clifford Bax, London: Home and Van That Ltd., 1946.

Ellen Terry and Bernard Shaw: *A Correspondence.* Edited by St. John Christopher, London: Constable and Co., 1931.

Shaw on Shakespeare. Edited and with an introduction by Edwin Wilson, London: Cassell, 1962.

Shaw on Theatre. Edited by E.J. West, New York: Hill and Wang, 1968.

The Complete Bernard Shaw—Plays and *The Complete Bernard Shaw—Prefaces.* London: Paul Hamlyn Ltd., 1965. (Printed in Czechoslovakia).

The Intelligent Woman's Guide to Socialism, Capitalism, Sovietism and Fascism. 2 Vols. London: Penguin Books Ltd., 1937.

The Matter with Ireland. Edited and with an introduction by David H. Green and Dan H. Lawrence, London: Rupert Hart—Davis, 1962.

The Sixteen Self-Sketches. London: Constable and Co., 1949.

What I Really Wrote about the War. London: Constable and Co., 1931.

SECONDARY SOURCES

Books

Adams, Ruth. *What Shaw Really Said.* London: Macdonald, 1966.

Amyot, Jackques. *Tudor Translations*. London: Everyman's Library, 1895.

Aristotle, *De Poetica*.Vol-XI. Edited by W.D. Ross, Oxford, 1910-31.

Ascham, Roger. *Sein Leben und Seine Werke*. Strasburg, 1879.

Asteley, Robert. *A History of English Classical Tragedies*. Oxford, 1912.

Athusser, Louis. *Lenin and Philosophy and other Essays*. Trans. Ben Brawster, London: New Left Books, 1971.

Bacon, Francis. *Historie and Chronicle*. London: John Murray, [fol. 10^{V}]; 1803.

Barclay, John. *Roman à Clef*. Argenis, 1617.

Barnett, S.A. (ed), *A Century of Darwin*. London: William Heinemann, 1959.

Barret, W.B. *The Trial of Jeanne d'Arc*. Trans. George Routledge & Kegan Paul, London: Trench Trubner and Co., 1931.

Bentley, Eric. *Bernard Shaw*. London: Robert Hale Ltd, 1950.

——. *The Cult of the Superman*. London: Robert Hale Ltd., 1947.

Bergson, H. *Creative Evolution*. Trans. Arthur Mitchell, New York: The Modern Library, 1964.

Berlin, Isiah. *Karl Marx—His Life and Environment*. London: Oxford University Press, 1951.

Bernanos, G. *Sanity will Out*. Trans. R. Bachelor, New York: Sheet and Ward, 1947.

Blundeville, *Storia della Storiografia*. n.p., Bari, 1917. Eng. Trans. Thomas Bogard, New York: Crofts, 1945.

Bogard, T. *Modern Drama* & W. Oliver, New York: Oxford University Press, 1965.

Bradbook, M.C. *Ibsen the Norwegian*. London: Chatto and Windus, 1948.

Brannigan, John. *New Historicism and Cultural Materialism*. New York: Transitions, 1990.

Brewster, David. *The Life of Sir Isaae Newton*. London: John Murray, 1831.

Butler, Samuel. *Evolution—Old and New.* Edition by R.A. Stratfield, London: A.C. Fifield, 1911.

Campbell, L.B. *Shakespeare's Histories.* London: Oxford University Press, 1964.

Carpenter, Charles. *Bernard Shaw and the Art of Destroying Ideals.* Madison: University of Wisconsin Press, 1969.

Carr, È.H. *What is History.* London: Macmillan, 1962.

Chaki, M.C. & N.C Bose Majumder, *Analytical Dynamics.* Kolkata: J.D. Library, 1987.

Charlton, G. *Shakespeare Politics and Politician.* Also in Besser als Shakespeare, Shakespeare Johrbuck, Lll, 1916.

Chesterton, G.K. *George Bernard Shaw.* London: The Bodley Head, 1950.

Cicero, *De Orator.* Bk-II, Loeb Classic Library, n.d.

Claire, Colebrook. *New Literary Histories.* Manchester: Manchester University Press, 1997.

Clark, G.N. *The Later Stuarts.* 1660-1714 London: Oxford University Press, 1934.

Cole, Toby. *Playwrights on Playwriting.* New York: Hill and Wang, 1960.

Colbourne, Maurice. *The Real Bernard Shaw.* London: J.M. Dent and Sons Ltd., 1949.

Coleridge, S.T. *Literary Remains.* Edited by H.N. Coleridge, London, 1836.

Collins, A.S. *English Literature of the Twentieth Century.* London: University Tutorial Press, 1951.

Collingwood, R.G. *The Idea of History.* London: Oxford University Press, 1951.

Coulton, G.G. *Inquisition and Liberty.* London: William Heinemann, 1938.

Croiset, *History de la Litierature Greequee.* English version, London: Oxford, 1908.

Crompton, Louis. *Shaw the Dramatist.* Nabraska: University of Nebraska Press, 1969.

Crose, *La Storia come Pensiero e come Azione*. English version, London, 1941.

Daiches, David. *A Critical History of English Literature*. Vol. II London: Secker and Warburg, 1960.

Danis, Leon. *The Mystery of Joan of Arc*. Trans. Arthur Conan Doyle, London: John Murray, 1924.

Danto, A.C. *Analytical Philosophy of History*. Cambridge: Cambridge University Press, 1966.

Darwin, Charles. *The Origin of Species*. Sixth edition. London: Oxford University Press, 1961.

Dey, P.K. *Eugene O' Neill—A Study of his Tragic Vision*. Bareilly: Prakash Book Depot, 2000.

Dietrich, R.F. *Portrait of the Artist as Young Superman*. Florida: University of Florida Press, 1969.

Duffin, Henry Charles. *The Quintessence of Bernard Shaw*. London: Allen and Unwin Ltd., 1920.

Durant, Will. *The Story of Civilization*. Part-III. New York: Simon and Schuster, 1944.

——. *The Story of Philosophy*. New York: Garden City, 1933.

Egerton, H.E. *A Short History of British Colonial Policy*. 1606-1909. London: Methuen, 1950.

Ervine, St. John. *Bernard Shaw: His Life, Work and Friends*. London: Constable and Co. Ltd., 1956.

Fabre, L. *Joan of Are*. Trans. Gerard Hopkins, London: Odhams Press Ltd., 1954.

Ferguson, W.K. and Mifflin. Houghton, *A Survey of European Civilization Since 1500*. Cambridge and Massachusetts: The Riverside Press, 1958.

Finger, Ben. *Concise World History*. London: Peter Owen, 1960.

Fowler, W.W. *Julius Caesar*. London: G.P. Putram Sons, 1928.

France, Anatole. *The Life of Joan of Arc*. Trans. Winifred Stephens and John Lane (in 3 Vols.), London: The Bodley Head Ltd., 1909.

Gallie, W.B. *Philosophy and the Historical Understanding.* London: Chatto and Windus, 1964.

Ganguly, S. and S. Das, *Analytical Dynamics of Particle.* Kolkata: New Central Book Agency, 2002.

Gelzer, M. *Caesar-Politician and Statesman.* Trans. Peter Needham and Basil Blackwell, Oxford, 1968.

Gibbs, A.M. *The Art and Mind of Shaw.* London: Macmillan, 1983.

Gower, L.R. *Joan of Arc.* London: John C. Nimmo, n.d.

Gray, Alexander. *The Socialist Tradition—Moses to Lenin.* London: Longmans, Green and Co., 1948.

Green, J.R. *A Short History of English People.* London: Macmillan, 1952.

Gustovson, C.G. *A Preface to History.* London: Mc Graw-Hill, 1955.

Hamilton, Paul. *Historicism.* London and New York: Routledge, 1996.

Hardy, A.C. and E.B. Ford, (eds.) *Evolution as a Process.* London: Allen and Unwin, 1964.

Harris, Frank. *Bernard Shaw.* London: Victor Gollancz Ltd., 1931.

Heywood, T. *An Apologie for Actors. Fol. F3* London, 1612.

Heitland, W.E. *A Short History of the Roman Republic.* Cambridge: Cambridge University Press, 1929.

Henderson, Archibald. *Bernard Shaw: Playboy and Prophet.* New York: D. Appleton and Co., 1932.

——. *George Barnard Shaw: The Man of the Century.* New York: Appleton Century Crofts 1nc. 1956.

Holroyd, Michael. *Bernard Shaw.* London: Chatto and Windus, 1935.

Holrayd, Michael (eds.), *The Genius of Shaw.* London: Hodder and Stoughten, 1969.

How and Wells, *Commentary on Herodotus.* Vol. I, Oxford, 1912.

Huang, Jolin. *Shaw and Galsworthy*. Norwood Edition, 1979.

Hugo, Leon. *Bernard Shaw: Playwright and Preacher*. London: Methuen, 1971.

Huizinga, J. Cousin, D.R., *A Definition of the Concepts of History*. Trans. Oxford, 1936.

Huxley, Julian. *Evolution in Action*. A Mentor Book, The New American Library, 1953.

Ibsen, Henric. *Eleven Plays of Henric Ibsen*. New York: The Modern Library, 1950.

Joad, C.E.M. *Shaw*. London: Victor Gollancz Ltd., 1949.

——. *Shaw and Society: An Anthology and a Symposium*. London: Odhams Press, 1951

——. *Matter, Life and Value*. London: Oxford University Press, 1929.

Kaufmann, R.J. (ed.) *G.B. Shaw: A Collection of Critical Essays*. New York: (Prentice) Hall, 1965.

Keith, Sir Arthur. *Essays on Human Evolution*. London: Watts and Co., 1947.

Lamark, Jean - Baptiste. *Zoological Philosophy*. Trans. Hugh Elliot, London: Macmillan, 1914.

Lang, A. *The Maid of France*. London: Longmans, Green and Co., 1929.

Langer, Lawrence. *G.B.S. and the Lunatic*. London: Hutchinson, 1964.

Lathrop, *Translation from the Classics*. London, Published between 1520-1523.

Lemon, L.T. *Approach to Literature*. New York: Oxford University Press, 1969.

Leonard, P. *A History of Scientific Progress*. London: G. Bell and Sons, 1933.

Liddell, H.G. *History of Rome*. London: John Murray, 1879.

Lightbody, C.W. *The Judgements of Joan*. London: Longmans, Green and Co., 1929.

Lockyer, Roger and David. Smith, *A History of England.* ELBS and Ernest Benn Ltd., 1952.

Lodge, R. *The Political History of England.* Vol. VIII, 1606-1702. London: Longmans, Green and Co., 1923.

Loney, S.L. *The Elements of Statics and Dynamics.* Cambridge: Cambridge University Press, 1988.

Ludwig, Emil. *Cleopatra, the Story of a Queen.* Trans. Bernard Miall, New York: Bantam Books, 1928.

——. *Nepoleon.* Trans. Eden and Cedar Paul, Munbai: Jaico Publishing House, 1987.

MacCarthy, Desmond, *Shaw.* London: Macgibbon and Kee, 1951.

Macardle, D. *The Irish Republic.* London: Victor Gollancz, 1937.

Macaulay, T.B. *The History of England.* Vol. I, Fifth Edition, London: Longmans, Brown, Green & Longman, 1849.

Mann, Thomas. *The Living Thoughts of Schopenhauer.* London: Cassel and Co., 1942.

Markham, Felix. *Nepoleon.* London: Weidenfield and Nicolson, 1964.

Marx, Karl. *Das Kapital.* Edited by Eden and Cedar Paul, London: George Allen and Unwin Ltd., 1929.

May, K.M. *Ibsen and Shaw, Part-II, Shaw.* London: Macmillan, 1956.

Mayne, Fred. *The Wit and Satire of Bernard Shaw.* London: Edward Arnold, 1967.

McCabe, Joseph. *George Bernard Shaw.* Noorwood, Pa. 1977.

Mommsen, Theodor. *The History of Rome.* Vol. V, Trans. William Purdie, Dickson, London: Macmillan, 1931.

Morgan, Margery M. *The Shavian Playground.* London: Methuen, 1972.

Murray, T.D. *Jeanne d'Arc.* London: Longmans, Green and Co., 1929.

Nicoll, Allardyce. *The Theory of Drama.* London: Geroge G. Harrap and Co. Ltd., 1937.

——. *British Drama.* London: George G. Harrap and Co. Ltd., 1967.

——. *A History of English Drama.* Vol. V. Cambridge: Cambridge University Press, 1959.

Nethercot, Arthur H. *Man and Superman: The Shavian Portrait Gallery.* Cambridge and Massachusetts: Harvard University Press, 1954.

Ohmann, Richard. *Shaw: the Style and the Man.* Weslyan University Press, 1962.

Paine, A.B. *The Girl in White Armour.* New York: Macmillan, 1927.

Pascal, Valerie. *The Disciple and the Devil.* London: Michael Joseph, 1971.

Patch, Blanche. *Thirty Years with G.B.S.* London: Victor Gollancz Ltd., 1951.

Pernoud, R. *The Retrial of Joan of Arc.* Trans. J.M. Cohen, London: Methuen, 1955.

Pearson, Hesketh. *G.B.S.: A Full-length Portrait.* New York: Garden City, 1946.

——. *G.B.S.A. Post-script.* London: Collins, 1951.

Plato, *The Republic.* Trans., Benjamin Jowett, Cleveland and New York: The World Publishing Co., 1964.

Plutarch, *Lives.* Trans., John and William Langhorne, London: Walter Scott Ltd., 1928.

Purdom, C.B. *A Guide to the Plays of Bernard Shaw.* London: Methuen, 1964.

Quintilian, *Institutes.* Bk-II, Stuttgart and Augsburg, 1858.

Rahman, M. *Rigid Dynamics.* Kolkata: New Central Book Agency, 2002.

Ramsey, A.S. *Dynamics. Part-I.* Cambridge: Cambridge University Press, Indian Edition, 1985.

Renier, G.J. *History—Its Purpose and Method.* London: George Allen and Unwin, 1950.

Resnick, R. and D. Halliday. *Physics. Part-I.* Wiley Eastern Ltd., Printed in India, 1960.

Rickman, H.P. (ed.) *Meaning of History*. London: Allen and Unwin, 1961.

Robertson, J.M., *Mr. Shaw and 'The Maid'*. London: Methuen, 1964.

Rose, J.H. *The Life of Napoleon. Tenth Edition*. London: G. Bell and Sons Ltd., 1929.

Roy, R.N. *George Bernard Shaw's Historical Plays*. Kolkata: A Mukherjee and Co. Pvt. Ltd., 1979.

Rosenblood, Norman. (ed.) *Shaw: Seven Critical Essays*. Toronto: University of Toronto Press, 1971.

Sackville, West Victorian. *Saint Joan of Arc*. London: Cobden—Sanderson, 1936.

Schelling, *The English Chronical Plays*. Oxford, 1902.

Scott, W.S. *The Trial of Joan*. London: The Folio Society, 1956.

Sengupta, S.C. *The Art of Bernard Shaw*. Kolkata: A Mukherjee and Co. Pvt. Ltd., 1974.

Simpson, G.G. *The Meaning of Evolution*. A Mentor Book, The American Library, 1948.

Smith, Gregory. *Elizabethan Critical Essays*. 2 Vols. Oxford, 1904.

Stewart, J.I.M. *Shaw, in Eight Modern Writers*. London: Oxford University Press, 1963.

Suetonius, T.G. *The Twelve Caesars*. Trans. Robert Graves, Penguin Books, 1958.

Thucydides, *The Pelopollesian War*. Trans. Jowett Benjamin in *The Greek Historian*, New York: Oxford University Press, 1942.

Tillyard, E.M.W. *Shakespeare's Historical Plays*. London: Chatto and Windus, 1959.

Trevelyan, G.M. *English Social History*. London: Longman, Green and Co. Ltd., 1948.

——. *History of England*. London: Longman, Green and Co. Ltd., 1945.

Trewin, J.C. *Dramatists of Today*. London: Oxford University Press, 1953.

Twain, Mark. *Personal Recollections of Joan of Arc*. Trans. Winifred Stephens, London: The Bodley Head, 1909.

Turco, Alfred. *Shaw's Moral Vision*. Ithaca: Cornell University Press, 1976.

Valency, Maurice. *The Cart and the Trumpet*. New York: Oxford University Press, 1973.

Waldman, Milton. *Joan of Arc*. Boston: Little Brown and Co., 1975.

Walsh, W.H. *Philosophy of History*. New York and End Evanston: Harper and Row, 1966.

Watson, Barbara. *A Shavian Guide to the Intelligent Women*. London: Chatto and Windus, 1964.

Wells, H.G. *The Outline of History*. London: Cassell and Co., 1956.

Wells, H.G., Julion Huxley and G.P. Wells. *The Science of Life*. London: Cassell and Co., 1931.

Wheeler, F.B. *The Story of Napoleon*. London: G. Harrap and Co., 1939.

Widagery, A.G. *Interpretations of History*. London: Allen and Unwin, 1961.

Williams, Raymond. *Drama from Ibsen to Eliot*. Penguin Books Inc., in association with Chatto and Windus; London, 1964.

Wilson, Colin. *Bernard Shaw: A Reassessment*. London: Hatchinson, 1964.

Winsten, S. *G.B.S. 90*. London: Hutchinson, 1964.

——. *Days with Bernard Shaw*. London: Huchinson, 1961.

Woodbridge, Homer. *Bernard Shaw: Creative Artist*. Carbondale: S. Illinois University Press, 1963.

Young, Hugh D. and Roger A. Freedman, *University Physics*. Massachusetts: Addison—Wesley, 1988.

Articles and Periodicals

Allencon, Nicholus. "History and The Maid." *Discover*, Mar, 1999: 72-73.

Ambirajan, S. Commentary on "The Contemporary History Handbook." *Hindu Book Review*, Tamil Nadu Edition, 1 June, 1999.

Eliot, T.S. "Shaw on Contemporary Theatre." *Criterion* [IV], April 1926: 389-390.

Henderson, A. "Caesar and Cleopatra." *New York Times*, New York Public Library Theatre Collection. 31 Oct. 1906.

Holsten, James. "Ranting at the New Historicism." *ELR*. 1989: 217-218.

McDowell, F.P.W. "Fountainhead and Fountain." *Shaw Review*, California, 1980: 187-190.

Meisel, Martin. "Cleopatra and 'The Flight into Egypt'". *Shaw Review*, California, May 1964: 72-76.

Shaw, G.B. "Given Caesar." *Academy*, 30 April, 1898: 121-128.

Shaw, G.B. Our Theatre in the Nineties. *New Statesmen*, 3 May, 1913: 112-113.

"Shaw and Comedy", Editorial. *Times*, 12 Aug. 1939, Late ed: A 15.

"The Bourgeois Revisionist." Editorial. *New York Herald,* 31 Oct. 1925, late ed.: A19.

Sylvan, B. "Bernard Shaw on Tragedy." *PMLA*, [LXXI], 888-889.

Weinthraub, Stonley. (ed.) *Annual of Bernard Shaw Studies*. Pennsylvania State University Press, 1983: 217-221.

West, E.J. "Shaw on Theatre." *New York Times*, 14 Sept., 1936: 87-92.

Chronology of Important Dates

1850	Shaw's father's civil service post in Dublin abolished.
1856	Shaw is born on 26th July in Dublin.
1859	Darwin's *Origin of Species* published.
1867	Shaw attends the first of his four Dublin Schools.
1867	Karl Marx's *Das Kapital* published.
1871	Darwin's *Descent of Man* published.
1875	Shaw's first contribution to the press.
1876	Leaves Dublin for London.
1879	Writes first novel, *Immaturity*.
1880	Writes second novel, *The Irrational Knot*.
1881	Writes third novel, *Love among the Artists*.
1882	Writes fourth novel, *Cashel Byron's Profession*.
1883	Writes fifth and last novel (incomplete), *An Unsocial Socialist*.
1884	Fabian Society founded.
1884	Joins Fabian Society.
1885	Reviews books for *Pall Mall Gazette* until 1888.
1885	His father dies. One of his speeches converts Annie Besant to Socialism.
1886	Writes Fabian articles for Annie Besant's *Our Corner*—Art Critic to *The World* until 1889.
1888	Music Critic for The Star until 1890 under the name of Corno di Bassetto.
1890	Music critic for *The World*.
1891	Writes *The Quintessence of Ibsenism*.

1892	First play, *Widower's House*, produced.
1893	Writes *The Philanderer.*
1893	Writes *Mrs. Warren's Profession.*
1894	Writes *Arms and the Man* and *Candida*. Shaw's first stage successes.
1895	Dramatic critic for *Saturday Review* until 1898.
1895	Writes *The Man of Destiny, You Never Can Tell* and *The Sanity of Art.*
1896	Writes *The Devil's Disciple.*
1896	Meets Charlotte Payne-Townshend, later Mrs. Shaw.
1898	Married Charlotte Payne-Townshend.
1898	Writes *Caesar* and *Cleopatra.*
1898	*Mrs. Warren's Profession* produced.
1898	*Plays, Pleasant and Unpleasant* published.
1899	Writes *Captain Brassbound's Conversion.*
1901-03	*Man and Superman* (produced in 1903), began Shaw's great period.
1901-03	First play to have a full-scale Shavian preface.
1904	Writes *John Bull's Other Island.*
1904	Writes *How He Lies to Her Husband.*
1904	Vedrenne-Barker management at Royal Court Theatre begins.
1905	Writes *Major Bardara.*
1906	Writes *The Doctor's Dilemma.* Bought "Shaw's Corner" at Ayot, St. Lawrence.
1908	Writes *Getting Married.*
1912	Writes *Androcles and the Lion.*
1912	Writes *Pygmalion.*
1914	Writes *Commonsense about the War.*
1920	Writes *Back to Methuselah.*
1920	*Heartbreak House* produced.
1923	Writes *Saint Joan.*

1925	Awarded Nobel Prize for Literature.
1928	The *Intelligent Woman's Guide to Capitalism and Socialism* published.
1929	Writes *The Apple Cart.*
1939	Writes *In Good King Charles's Golden Days.*
1943	Mrs. Shaw died.
1947	Writes his last complete play at the age of 91, Byoyant Billion.
1950	Shaw died at his home in Ayot, St. Lawrence, November 2nd·

Index